Diana Wright is the Personal [...] of *The Sunday Times*. Her p[...] include *A Guide to Mortgage[...] Lump Sum Investment* and *A History of the SS Great Britain*. In 1995 she was awarded a Golden Pen Award for Personal Finance Journalism sponsored by the Co-operative Bank, being voted the Journalists' Journalist of the Year.

Diana Wright is the series editor for *The Sunday Times Personal Finance Guides*.

THE SUNDAY TIMES
Personal Finance Guide to

YOUR
RETIREMENT

How to Plan Wisely for Later Life

Diana Wright

HarperCollins*Publishers*

HarperCollins*Publishers*,
77–85 Fulham Palace Road,
Hammersmith, London W6 8JB

A Paperback Original 1996
5 7 9 8 6 4

A catalogue record for this book
is available from the British Library

ISBN 0 00 638707 1

Set in Linotron Times by
Rowland Phototypesetting Limited,
Bury St Edmunds, Suffolk

Printed and bound in Great Britain by
Caledonian International Book Manufacturing Limited, Glasgow

CONTENTS

ACKNOWLEDGEMENTS

I would like to thank the following people and companies for their help in preparing this book: Pensions experts Ron Spill of Legal & General and Steve Bee of Prudential; William Burrows of Annuity Direct and Peter Quinton of the Annuity Bureau; the helpful press teams at the Benefits Agency and the Inland Revenue and, in particular, Rachel Dunachie of the Benefits Agency and Paul Franklin at the Inland Revenue.

In addition, I would like to thank the firms of independent advisers or stockbrokers who contributed to solving the investment problems described in Chapter 11: Amanda Davidson of Holden Meehan, Peter Hargreaves of Hargreaves Lansdown, Danby Bloch of Raymond Godfrey and Partners, Michael Otway of Carr Sheppards and Vanessa Barnes of Chase de Vere Investments.

INTRODUCTION
How to Handle Your Money in Retirement

This book will not tell you how to have a happy retirement, but it will help you to ensure that it is, as far as possible, a financially comfortable one.

Most people do not want to spend long hours contemplating money problems – or even money solutions; after all, there are many more interesting things to think about. But when we retire our lives change dramatically; part of this change will be financial so it is essential to make plans for the future. A burst of activity now should stand you in good stead later. This guide aims to help you to get your affairs on to a sound footing for your retirement so that you will not be forced to spend countless hours in the future thinking, or worrying, about your finances.

That said, some people enjoy managing their investments; as with so many other things in life, the more you know, the more interesting it becomes, but you will need to cover a certain amount of groundwork first. And if you are not an 'investment hobbyist', then this book should certainly be essential reading.

For many people, understandably, retirement can appear to pose more anxieties than enticing opportunities. Those retiring from a good company pension scheme may have access to a significant lump sum, probably the largest they have ever had to deal with in their lives. The temptation is to put it somewhere 'safe' (usually a building society account) on the basis that they cannot afford to lose it. This may or may not be the most sensible thing to do; it may even – depending on your circumstances – turn out to be positively imprudent. The vital decisions to be taken at this stage in life may well intimidate you. When you are working you can always use next month's pay cheque to help you out of temporary difficulties, or save hard for the next year or two to rebuild your nest-egg after a financial setback: when you are retired this is no longer possible.

Within the vast financial services industry there are large numbers of people with considerable experience, knowledge and judgement. They are there to help you, but many of our readers' letters show that people are, by and large, unwilling to put their trust wholeheartedly in someone they have never met before – particularly on such an important issue. They are just not confident enough of being able to spot good advice from bad.

Some parts of the industry have attracted bad publicity in recent years: advice given has sometimes proved to be more in the interest of the salesman than the client. But don't be put off from taking any advice because of this. There *is* a way round the problem: make sure you do sufficient groundwork yourself so that you know, broadly, what it is you are seeking and can recognize sensible advice.

The book contains some specific examples of investment problems and how they might be approached. The time-lag between writing and publishing means that some factors, such as interest rates, may well have changed, but the process is generally slower than we imagine: the inflation rate may rise or fall month by month but it's unlikely to double, or to halve; interest rates may be pushed up (or down) half a point or more, but the broad relationship between inflation, interest rates and other potential returns tends to remain reasonably steady for many years at a time.

However, you should bear in mind that these examples are just that – examples – not recommendations on specific courses of action. They should give you an idea of how problems can be tackled, and provide a rough benchmark against which you can judge whatever up-to-date, specific advice you may be given.

Planning of any sort means trying to predict the future, and adjusting present-day actions in the light of those plans. Retirement planning involves (no use beating about the bush!) making a guess at how long you are likely to last. Life expectancy tables make unexpectedly cheery reading: the older you get, the longer still you are likely to live. These tables, worked out by life insurance companies for their own ends, don't run out completely until the age of 109, at which point women still have an average life expectation of 0.862 years (though mere males peter out at the age of 108).

Table 1 shows the average expectation of life from age 55 – the point at which an increasing number of people start thinking about 'early retirement'. Those trying to work out how to stretch their money over the rest of their lives must conclude from this table that, unlike Charles II, who supposedly apologized on his death-bed for taking 'an unconscionable time dying', we spend an unconscionable time living.

Table 1: Average life expectancy

Age now	Average future life expectancy (years)	
	Male	Female
55	20.135	25.025
60	16.383	20.890
65	13.036	17.010
70	10.123	13.414
75	7.699	10.207
80	5.782	7.495
85	4.345	5.381
90	3.331	3.949

Source: M&G Re

As the years roll by, these tables need adjusting in the light of actual experience, and so far the trend has been in one direction only – upwards. In 1910, for example, only 189 out of every 1,000 men aged 50 could expect to survive to age 80; today, more than 300 will celebrate their 80th birthday. Similarly, 315 out of every 1,000 women aged 50 in 1932 could expect to reach 80, while today the proportion is around 53%. Even at age 80, assuming they chose their parents sufficiently wisely, 50% of men and 70% of women can look forward to reaching 85, and one in five men (more than one in three women) will reach 90. And such is the progress made by medical science that even if you are confident now that you're going to pop off well before the age of 80, you can't rely on it – some new miracle cure could upset all your predictions.

All in all, then, your money in retirement must really earn its keep. If you are a long-term member of a good company pension scheme, much – though not necessarily all – of that burden will be off your hands; but this is something that you cannot change at this stage in the game – any more than you can change your parents. But whatever your circumstances, some careful planning at this stage should improve your long-term prospects. I hope this book will help you to do just that.

1 | *Planning Your Retirement: the Groundwork*

Some people can hardly wait for their retirement, while others put off even thinking about it until the day arrives.

If you're self-employed, of course, you can just carry on working, putting off the 'evil' day more or less indefinitely – although your partner may not be quite so happy with that arrangement. Even the most well-balanced individual is likely to approach with feelings of both joy and trepidation a landmark which for most of us represents the biggest change to our lives since the day we left school or started our first job. Being a 'learner' again after 30 or 40 years is an unsettling experience – as anyone who has finally learned to drive in middle age can testify.

Major financial changes after retirement may well be uppermost in people's minds; if you think about and plan your finances you may well find yourself considering your broader situation in retirement. Ideally, you should start some serious planning a few years before the big day. If you are fortunate, you can construct your own timetable, although in recent years many people have had 'early retirement' thrust upon them as companies have ruthlessly cut out layers of management under the impact of the recession.

Timetable for Your Retirement

Five years to go
- Consider whether you want to make any major structural alterations to your home. If so, embark on them now – get the mess out of the way before you're at home all day.
- Carry out a first check on the amount of pension you

are likely to receive: start additional pension savings if necessary.

- Will your mortgage be fully paid off by the time you retire? If not, consider making extra payments from now to ensure that it is.
- If you do not have one already, take out a Tax Exempt Special Savings Account (Tessa) – it will mature in five years' time to give you an extra treat on retirement.

Four years to go

- Monitor your credit and store card spending. Running up debts on credit cards is a luxury for busy people with more money than sense (or time). If you habitually carry forward a large debit balance on your cards, start clearing it to ensure you are debt-free by retirement day. Likewise with any hire purchase agreements or bank overdrafts.

Three years to go

- Feeling the first inkling of the potentialities of life after work? Time to stock up on the kit for those hobbies you will soon be able to pursue: buy the camera (or whatever) you have always promised yourself.
- Get tough with offspring – get them to clear out 'their' bedrooms and nab them for your darkroom, study or general 'hobby' room. (It will probably take at least three years for your edict to be obeyed, so issue it at once. Threaten to burn cherished collections of Action Men and Sindy dolls; in the last resort, carry it out.)

Two years to go

- Carry out a house stock-taking exercise. Repairs and refurbishments should be carried out now, paying particular attention to the effect these might have on running costs. So, for instance, it may be worth replacing the central heating boiler, improving the insulation, or installing double glazing now.

- Run an eye over the rest of your white and brown goods – the washing machine, fridge, freezer, television, video and so on – and consider replacing if they are becoming long in the tooth.
- Do you still rent your telephones? It's an easy matter to overlook as the rental is small compared to overall bills. But buying your own means one less item of expense after retirement.
- Check your pension situation once again. Increase pension savings if appropriate and possible. If you are already saving the maximum allowed, use Personal Equity Plans to build up a store of tax-free investments.

One year to go
- Time to look at transport. Do you drive a company car? Start considering how you will replace it. Even if you don't, consider whether you should be changing from an expensive-to-run status symbol to a cheaper, nippy run-about. Think about 'downsizing' from two cars to one – and buy a couple of bicycles, for sheer enjoyment as well as convenience and economy.
- Consider your post-retirement taxation position. Now that you have a fairly clear idea of how much your pension is going to be, consider juggling any other investments you might hold to make use of separate taxation. If one partner has only a small income (or perhaps none) in their own right, he or she should be the one to hold the bulk of your combined income-producing investments.
- Start making a monthly budget of the typical 'running costs' of your life. If you are married, this needs to be a joint exercise; one of you may have been meeting regular costs that the other has no knowledge of – for instance, the window cleaner, the gardener, the newspaper bill. Your overall 'running costs' will inevitably change after retirement, because the nature of your life will change – but at

least such an exercise should provide an initial yardstick for you.

Costs of Life After Retirement

No great financial acumen is required to work out the principal changes in costs after retirement: up will go heating and lighting, possibly car (if you had a company one before), and increased leisure expenditure; down will go 'smart' clothes (previously needed for work), lunching out, and commuting costs.

You may, however, be tripped up by some of the less obvious changes, for instance:

Up
- Telephone bills, now that you can no longer phone from work
- Small treats – cream tea at a country café, for instance, formerly restricted to weekends
- Daily tea and coffee for the caffeine addicts
- Paper, pens, paperclips, photocopying, stamps – not, of course, that you made a habit of using the office mailbag for private post, but . . .

Happily, most of these extra expenses are relative molehills in a well-ordered budget. In any case, you might not have thought of some surprising falls in running costs, such as:

Down
- Premiums for home contents insurance, now that the house is occupied all day
- Premiums on car insurance, often available for 'safer' older drivers
- Current account costs, as you have the time to seek out the best deal
- Food – with less need for expensive convenience meals and time to 'pick your own' – indeed, to 'grow your own' – you could find that the weekly food bill diminishes.

Of course, it is not easy to generalize about the effect of retirement on household budgets because each of us is different; how much we spend, and on what, is an individual reflection of who we are as well as our overall means. But you may find it difficult to predict precisely how your spending patterns will change once you reach retirement. Until you have adjusted to your new way of life, you won't know yourself. However, those who have gone through the process find that, during the first year of retirement, spending – particularly on 'leisure' – seems to rise dramatically. Don't panic if this happens because it rarely continues at this rate. I suspect that, during the first year of adjustment, people find that time hangs heavy on their hands, and money is inevitably required to fill the holes. As they adjust to a different time-scale in life and embark on voluntary work or social activities close to their home-base, such spending tends to fall away.

Budget Planning Points

Current accounts
Most banks these days offer current accounts which pay interest on credit balances – though rates as low as 0.2% per year are scarcely the route to riches. Nevertheless, it will be worth casting an eye over your banking arrangements on retirement: you may prefer to move your account to a branch near your home; it may be simpler to run one joint account rather than two individual ones (or vice versa). Finally, you might have chosen your existing account because of the beneficial conditions it offered to people who habitually dip into the red. After retirement you will probably both wish and need to run your affairs more tightly, in which case a different account may be more suitable.

Plastic
This is also a good time to count up just how many credit cards or store cards you have accumulated over your working life. One is

really quite sufficient for most people – and it may be possible to get one free of any annual fee (with a second card available on the same account thrown in). Some of the 'free' card issuers often turn down applicants: don't interpret this as a slur on your credit-worthiness – rather the reverse (those who pay off their balance in full each month are the least attractive customers from the issuer's point of view). Secure a new card before getting rid of all your old ones.

Store cards, with the exception of the John Lewis card, tend to have even higher rates of interest than credit cards, so if you do wish to keep them, make sure that they are used purely as a means of payment and not as a vehicle for credit. Finally on the plastic front, the charge cards, such as those issued by American Express and Diners Club, usually have the highest annual fees of all, and this may be the appropriate time to let them go.

Insurance
Insurance companies have begun to realize that older people are better customers because they tend to make fewer claims ('older' generally means over 55), so if you have not done so already, do look at your general insurance arrangements. Some leg-work in the area of car and contents insurance could lead to cuts in premiums of at least 5 to 10%. (Buildings insurance premiums are not affected by the age of the policyholder, but there may still be savings to be made, particularly if you have stayed with the policy originally sold to you by your building society many years ago.)

As regards house contents and car insurance, older people are quite simply a better bet; they are safer and steadier drivers, more honest in making claims and, when they are not clocking up their limited mileage by driving gently down the high street, they tend to be at home, deterring the opportunistic burglar simply by their presence. All these factors cut the risk of claims on such policies quite significantly – so premiums should be lower. And however remote this identikit picture might be from you as an individual, the fact that you have reached that certain age should allow you to qualify for these reductions, assuming a reasonable claims record.

There are various routes to obtaining cheaper insurance. One is to shop around by contacting the 'direct' insurers which only deal over the telephone; the second is to go to an ordinary insurace broker or intermediary; and the third, to contact the specialists in the retired market. The charity Age Concern, for instance, has an insurance services division, and there are some other brokers specializing in the 'retired' market. Details of useful addresses are shown in Appendix I (see page 161).

Carrying out an exhaustive 'shop around' can be an extremely lengthy process. However, it will almost certainly be worth consulting at least one intermediary and contacting two or three of the 'direct' insurers. And don't forget to ask your existing insurer whether it has any special deals for the retired. Home contents policies are beginning to offer 'no claims discounts' to their policyholders, but unlike motor insurance, these cannot be transferred to a new company.

Your mortgage

Many people will have finished paying off their mortgage well before the time they retire. If you are within the last few years of the term, consider accelerating the payment so as to clear it fully by that time. While mortgage interest still attracts some tax relief in relation to capital sums of £30,000 or less, the value of this has diminished steadily over the years. Currently relief is available at the rate of 15%. This means that the basic variable mortgage rate of around 8% gross (late 1995) nets down to 6.8%. Any building society income you receive on which you pay basic-rate tax will be at a lower rate than this – so if you have surplus cash from this source, it would be wise to use it on the mortgage.

You should certainly try to pay off the outstanding sum if you are within three or four years of the end of a 25-year repayment mortgage. Most lenders 'load' their interest on at the beginning of the year, by reference to the capital sum outstanding at that time and irrespective of the fact that you will be paying capital off during the following 12 months. So you are, in effect, 'overpaying' interest. In the early years of a loan, the difference is tiny, because the bulk of each monthly payment goes to meet the interest and only a small proportion repays the capital. In the later years, however, the position is reversed and most of each monthly payment represents capital. It is therefore worthwhile paying off the balance of the capital owed early. If you have no particular desire to look after your own title deeds, you may be able to leave them with your lender by keeping a nominal £1 debt on the mortgage.

Home improvements

Before paying off the mortgage, however, consider whether you will wish at a later stage to take out a loan for some major home improvements. Such loans no longer qualify for any tax relief at all, so it is worth keeping your ready cash for this purpose and continuing with the mortgage.

Moving

The situation with regard to tax relief on interest also has implications for those planning to move house on retirement. You will probably be in a position to pay cash for it, but there may be a case for taking out a small mortgage (up to £30,000) even if you do not need to. Because you will get the tax relief on a loan taken out for purchase but not on one for improvements, if you plan to carry out improvements, they should be funded by your new mortgage, rather than a later bank loan.

Pre-retirement portfolio planning

There is little point in rearranging your investment portfolio wholesale before you need to, and often good reason to delay. While you are earning, you may be subject to the top 40% tax rate, which will make certain types of investment more suitable than others; on retirement, you may drop to a lower rate, which will shift the balance.

As a general rule, however, do not feel you must reorganize your portfolio overnight. If you are shifting substantial sums of money from one asset class to another, there is always the risk that you might get the timing wrong and sell out of company shares just when the market is particularly low, for example. If you have a good financial adviser, take his or her advice on when it is appropriate to turn equity investments into cash. A delay of a few months or a year or two after retirement may turn out to be wise.

The most important thing you can do in the sphere of 'pre-retirement' investment is to ensure – where possible – that you are using the maximum annual allowances for Personal Equity Plans. Individuals can invest up to £9,000 per year in these plans, but the allowance cannot be carried forward if you do not make full use of it. Those with large portfolios should aim to use the allowances each year without fail so that as high a proportion as possible of their assets is held within a Pep.

2 ‖ Pensions from the State: What They Provide, When, and How to Get Them

Planning your retirement finances must start with pensions, and for many people that will mean at least two sources of income: pensions from the State, and a pension from one or more previous employers. This chapter looks at the various State pension schemes; for company and personal pensions, see Chapters 3 to 5 (pages 24 to 66).

There are three main types of State pension you may be eligible for: the basic Retirement Pension, payable to all who have paid or been credited with sufficient National Insurance Contributions (NICs); the State Earnings Related Pension Scheme (SERPS), for which you may or may not be eligible; and the Graduated Retirement Benefit, which goes to people who paid graduated NICs at any time between April 1961 and April 1975.

The Basic Pension

The basic pension is increased in April each year in ilne with price inflation.

For the tax year April 1995 to April 1996 the full pension is:

£3,075.80 for a single person
£4,911.40 for a married couple

For the tax year April 1996 to April 1997, the full pension is:

£3,179.80 for a single person
£5,083.00 for a married couple

There is also, currently, a Christmas bonus of £10 tax-free, and pensioners over 80 automatically get an increase, currently 25p a week. The pension is payable weekly from age 65 (men) and 60 (women). The retirement age for women is set to increase, eventually, to match men's, but the change is to be phased in over a number of years starting in 2010. This means the changes will not in any way affect women born before 6 April 1950.

Those who are well off may view the basic old age pension as a very small part of their overall planning, but to put it into context, a man would need to invest a capital sum of just over £60,000 to provide the equivalent of the married couple's pension of £4,911. For a single woman retiring at 60, the equivalent capital sum required to produce the single person's pension of £3,075.80 is still around £50,000, thanks to the earlier start date and women's greater expectation of life.

Who gets the basic pension?
Anyone who has paid or been credited with sufficient NI contributions of the right sort – roughly 90% of the theoretical maximum – is entitled to the full basic pension. Those who have paid less get less; in some circumstances, it is possible to make up the difference by paying extra contributions before retirement. To qualify at all, you do need to have actually paid some NI contributions at some time in the past – either a full year's worth (April to April) after 1975, or a total of 50 weekly contributions before then.

How to claim
Anyone who has paid sufficient gets the single person's pension; married women who have worked only a little or not at all can get a pension based on their husband's contributions. If he qualifies for the maximum, he would receive the single person's pension of £3,075.80 and she would receive the maximum 'dependant's addition' of £1,835.60, which adds up to £4,911.40 – in other words, the 'married' pension. For the 1996–97 tax year, the relevant

figures are £3,179.80 for the single person's pension and £1,903.20 for the dependant's addition.

The Department of Social Security should send you a claim form (BR1) a few months before you reach retirement age. If you do not receive it within, say, three months of your relevant birthday, you should contact them.

How the system works

The small print is complicated, partly because the government has chopped and changed its rules on National Insurance and pension schemes several times during the life of anyone coming up for retirement today, but also because any system which tries to be 'fair' in a range of different circumstances is bound to involve all sorts of special rules. For full details of pensions and other State benefits you will need the following booklets, usually available in post offices, local Social Security offices, Citizen's Advice Bureaux and so on:

FB6: *Retiring? Your Pension and Other Benefits*
NP46: *A Guide to Retirement Pensions*

The following booklets may also be useful:

NI184: *Over 80 Pension*
NI92: *Giving Up Your Right to Retirement Pension to Earn Extra*
FB32: *Benefits After Retirement*
FB2: *Which Benefit?*
CA01: *National Insurance Contributions: for Employees*
CA07: *National Insurance Contributions: Unpaid and Late Paid Contributions*
CA08: *National Insurance Contributions: Voluntary Contributions*

There is also a telephone advice service (Freeline Social Security on 0800 666 555) which will give general information, but not information specific to your circumstances.

The system works by establishing the number of years of your 'working life' – 49 for a man (except for a few men retiring in 1996, when it may be a little lower), and 44 for a woman. The amount of pension you get then depends on the number of 'qualifying' years for which you have paid or been credited with the appropriate class of NICs.

A record of approximately 90%, as indicated above, will qualify you for the full pension. Below this number, there is a sliding scale. Booklet NP46 (table 3) gives full details; Table 2 provides a summary.

Table 2: How much of the basic pension will you qualify for?

WOMEN		MEN	
Number of qualifying years	*% of pension*	*Number of qualifying years*	*% of pension*
0–9	NIL	0–10	NIL
10	26%	11	25%
15	39%	15	35%
20	52%	20	46%
25	65%	25	57%
30	77%	30	69%
35	90%	35	80%
39 & upwards	100%	40	91%
		44 & upwards	100%

Married women who have not worked all that much may well be better off claiming on their husband's contribution record. This calculation will be carried out automatically. Sometimes they can get a mixture – a small pension in their own right plus a pension based on their husband's record.

In some circumstances you may receive a higher pension than this table seems to suggest. For instance, although the working life starts notionally at age 16 for both men and women, children still at school until they are 18 can be credited as if they had paid the appropriate NI contributions, and so these count as qualifying years. Students in higher education, incidentally, are not credited in this way. They can catch up later by paying Voluntary Class 3 contributions, but there is a time limit of six years after the end of their course.

Women – or men – who have taken time off from work to bring up children, or to look after someone else who is sick or disabled, may receive 'Home Responsibilities Protection' (HRP). This means they need fewer qualifying years to get a full pension: a minimum of 20 qualifying years are required for a full pension in these circumstances, if they have sufficient HRP years under their belt, while a lower number will provide a reduced pension. (In fact, you do not actually have to have stayed at home during the HRP years – you might have worked on a temporary basis from time to time without staying long enough to build up a record of qualifying years by paying NICs throughout a tax year.) You should note, however, that HRP is not awarded for any tax year before 1978–79.

You should have been given HRP automatically for any full tax year in which you got Child Benefit, or Income Support for looking after someone sick or disabled (if you hadn't paid enough NICs to qualify). But note that it has to be you, not your partner, who received the Child Benefit. In other circumstances, you might need to apply for HRP (you need form CF411, available from local Social Security offices).

How to find your way around the rules
This is only a summary of a fairly labyrinthine system. While it may be useful to understand the basics, the relevant Government offices will do the specific calculations for you. The best thing to do is to obtain a 'pension forecast' a few years before retirement, as it may be possible to pay extra NI contributions now to increase the pension entitlement. There is a time limit in respect of missed contributions of six years, so even if you are still a few years away from retirement, it may be worth doing so sooner rather than later.

To obtain the pension forecast, you must complete form BR19, available from the local Social Security office. The forecast is based on your current contribution record. It can be requested at any time up to 4 months before the State retirement ages (60 for women, 65 for men until 2010).

If your record is patchy, the local office will tell you if it is possible for you to make voluntary contributions now – bearing in mind the six-year rule – and if so, how much is required. CA07, *Unpaid and Late Paid Contributions*, is the relevant booklet.

Continuing to work after retirement

If you do not in fact retire at the minimum State retirement pension age (65 for a man, 60 for a woman) the good news is that you do not have to pay any more NI contributions (although an employer must continue to pay its share). For the self-employed, liability for Class 2 contributions ceases immediately after your birthday (60th for women and 65th for men). For Class 4 contributions, liability ceases from the start of the following tax year.

You can, if you wish, put off receiving the State pension for five years after that date. If you do, your entitlement will usually be increased by around 7.5% for each year you put it off (with pro-rata increases for shorter terms), except when you are receiving some other State benefit. Arithmetically, it probably makes more sense to take it anyway and, if you don't need the money, invest it – but if you currently pay tax at the higher rate of 40%, and expect to fall back to a lower rate after you finally retire, you may be better off deferring the State pension until your tax rate falls.

Some people may retire from their 'proper' job at the State retirement age, but then start up in business as a self-employed consultant, making them eligible to save in a personal pension. It may be a good idea at this point to take the State pension at the earliest possible date and to reinvest it in a personal pension for five years, as the following example shows.

Andrew Marvell retired – as an employee – on his 65th birthday in August 1995, and immediately set up an advisory consultancy working principally for his old company for an annual fee of £15,000. He intends, and expects, to carry on working in this capacity for five years. He faces a choice on what to do with his State pension: either defer taking it, in which case it will grow by 7.5% for each year of deferment, or take it now and invest it in a personal pension.

	Deferring the pension	Taking and investing it
Current income from pension:	Nil	£58.85 a week – invested in a personal pension plan
Extra income in 5 years' time:	£22 a week	£40.96 a week *or* lump sum of £4,200 plus £30.77 a week

Note: *investing is a good move for Andrew, but it won't be for everyone. First, he is determined to continue working for a full five years. If he were to stop after just a year or two, the set-up charges on the personal pension could outweigh the advantages. Second, he is still earning a reasonable income from work. Under tax regulations, he cannot save more than 40% of his 'net relevant earnings' (the taxable profit from his consultancy) in a pension plan; if his annual earnings had been less than £8,743 he would not be allowed to save the full amount of his weekly State pension.*

The personal pension figures also assume the investments will grow by 9% a year – they might well grow more slowly, in which case his 'profit' compared with deferring the State pension will be lower.

Source: Prudential

Retiring before State pension age

If you retire before the age of 60 you should consult your Social Security office: you may be advised to pay voluntary NI contributions (Class 3) to protect your pension entitlement. However, men who retire after they have reached 60 but before 65 will have contributions automatically credited.

Graduated Retirement Benefit

This was a State scheme which ran from 1961 to 1975; anyone who paid NI contributions during this time and was earning more than about £9 a week will probably get a small graduated pension based on these contributions, but the overall amounts will be small because the scheme made no allowance for inflation; the maximum will be no more than about £5.50 to £6.50 a week. Once payments have started, they will be uprated each year in line with inflation. Any amounts due under this scheme will be included in the pension forecast provided by the Social Security office.

State Earnings Related Pension Scheme (Serps)

Serps arrived in April 1978 and is still with us, although many people are automatically 'contracted out' of the scheme through their membership of a company pension scheme, and others have been encouraged to contract out by changes implemented by the Government since the late 1980s. The self-employed are also largely excluded.

Who gets it?
Employees who have paid the full rate, Class I NICs on a specific band of earnings for the whole of any tax year since April 1978 are eligible for some Serps entitlement. The self-employed are basically excluded from Serps (in some cases there may be a very small entitlement).

How much do you get?
This depends, first, on when you are retiring. If it is before April 1999, the following rules apply; after that the amounts will be scaled down.

Serps is designed as a top-up to the basic retirement pension; it relates to a specific band of earnings, between a 'lower level' and an 'upper level' – the lower level is the same as a full single person's pension, and the upper level, roughly seven times that. They are increased each year to keep pace with the pension. For 1995–96, they are, respectively, £58 a week and £440 a week and for 1996–97, £61 a week and £455 a week. Any amounts you earn above the upper level are 'wasted' as far as Serps is concerned.

The amount you get depends on the total amount of your earnings between these two levels for each tax year since 1978. The calculation is fairly mind-boggling. Basically, what happens is this: your earnings for each year are increased in line with the increase in the national average earnings since you received them, and then the qualifying level for the basic pension is knocked off each figure. Then you add together everything that is left, divide the result by 80 – and that is your annual Serps pension.

The current maximum amount (from April 1995) is £84.61 a week. The pension forecast (see page 18 above) will, thankfully, include a calculation of any sums due under the Serps scheme. Serps pensions, like the other State pensions, are increased in line with price inflation once they start being paid.

Widows and widowers

The current rules are that a widow is entitled to all her husband's Serps regardless of their ages when he died. If she has her own Serps entitlement after retirement, she gets both, subject to an overall maximum.

A widower can receive his wife's Serps entitlement only if they were both over pensionable age when she died. Again, he may also have his own, subject to an overall maximum.

State Pensions and Income Tax

Tax is never deducted from State pensions. This does not, of course, mean that they are tax-free, although if the basic pension is your sole income, it will be covered by your annual tax-free allowance. However, where a wife is more than five years younger than her husband, the dependant's addition of £1,903.20 counts as the husband's income (and is therefore taxable as his) until she reaches 60. Once she passes that age, it is treated as her income, and can be set against her tax-free allowance.

The State pension is still by far the largest source of income for most people over retirement age – and given that the single pension amounts to no more than 18% of national average earnings these days, you can see just how little most pensioners have to live on. However, many people are in the fortunate position of being able to expect a decent income from a company pension. These are dealt with in the following chapter.

3 || *Company Pensions*

If you have already retired, you can skip the next few chapters. But if you are still a year or two away from the big day, you may need answers to many of the following questions.

- How much is my pension likely to be?
- If I take early retirement, how will my pension be affected?
- How can I trace pension entitlements from companies I have worked for in the past?
- Are there any sensible 'last minute' moves I can make to increase my pension?
- What should I do with the tax-free cash – take it, or take the pension?
- If I do take the cash, how much will it be – and by how much will it reduce my pension?
- What if I decide to carry on working, maybe as a self-employed consultant?

The aim of this and the following chapters is to answer all these questions as far as possible, or at least to point you in the right direction.

How Much Will My Pension Be?

Until you have got a reasonably accurate answer to this question, you can hardly embark on any other financial planning. A few people will be able to find out the answer with no difficulty. If you have worked for the same company all your life, and that company has a good final salary-type pension scheme, then you will probably get a pension of something close to two-thirds your final salary. Whether it is exactly two-thirds, or something less, and whether, for example, the pension will be flat or index-linked, are matters you can find out easily enough by reading the scheme booklet or ringing your employer's pensions department.

For most people, the answer is likely to be less clear-cut. There are two very different types of pension plan in existence: the first, to which the majority of employees belong, is labelled a 'final salary' scheme; the second, which covers all personal and self-employed pensions, and also certain company schemes run in a similar fashion, is known as a 'money purchase' scheme. It is quite possible that someone with a varied employment record will have accumulated pension rights under both types of scheme. Translating those rights into reasonably accurate estimates of actual post-retirement income requires two quite different approaches.

Final Salary Schemes

A final salary scheme gives employees a fraction of their final salary on retirement for each year they have worked for the company. Under Inland Revenue rules, the absolute maximum pension that can be granted is two-thirds final salary, which requires a minimum length of service of either 10 or 20 years, depending on the rules in force when you joined your scheme. Widow's (or widower's) pensions of up to two-thirds the employee's own pension may be paid after the employee's death. All pensions can be fully index-linked to the rise in prices.

That is the maximum according to the Inland Revenue; but most 'good' company schemes in fact use a fraction of one 60th of final salary for each year of service, providing a two-thirds pension only after 40 years' service. Employees can increase their entitlement (within the overall maximum) by saving additional amounts in a scheme known as Additional Voluntary Contributions or AVCs, which is a particularly useful facility for people whose working lives are shorter than 40 years.

Out of this total entitlement employees can, if they wish,

'commute' (i.e. change) a portion into a tax-free cash sum, available on retirement. The theoretical maximum here is one and a half times their final salary, available after 20 years' service – though in practice most schemes provide this only after 40 years' service. Someone with the appropriate length of service retiring on £40,000, say, could get tax-free cash of £60,000, and a reduced pension.

These rules on the maximum pension and cash sum available are extremely complicated, and depend in part on precisely when you joined your scheme. The section at the end of this chapter gives fuller details (see page 40).

The big exception within this final salary-type of scheme are those run for civil servants and employees of other governmental or quasi-governmental organizations (including nationalized industries and some of their privatized successors), who typically get one 80th of final salary for each year worked – which appears rather less generous – but they get a tax-free cash sum of up to one and a half times final salary *in addition to* the pension. On a rough and ready calculation this comes to much the same thing as a company one 60th scheme. The other main difference is that Government pensions are usually guaranteed to rise in line with inflation; while many big company schemes undertake to try to match inflation (and at today's rates, many are in fact doing so), few offer a cast-iron guarantee.

All these maximum rules may be subject to the earnings 'cap', a rule which applies to people who joined their schemes after June 1989. This rule stated that the maximum salary that could be taken into account for the purpose of pension schemes was £60,000, an amount which is usually increased by inflation each year. In the 1995–96 tax year the 'cap' stood at £78,600, and in the current (1996–97) tax year, at £82,200.

Anyone earning above that amount can still save for their retirement and, indeed, still benefit from employers' contributions, but there is no tax relief available on such savings, and employees must pay tax on any such contributions made on their behalf by their company. What companies do for their high-earning employees in this situation varies on a case-by-case basis – it could well depend on the extent of your individual negotiating clout with your employer. If you are in such a situation, it might be worth getting professional advice from a firm of consulting actuaries (although this may come with a hefty price tag attached).

When the cap was brought in it was not made retrospective. So if you have been a member of the same pension scheme since before 1989, the cap does not apply to you – as long as you don't change your job before retirement. There may also be a limit on the amount that can be taken as tax-free cash, again depending on when you joined the scheme. Further details of the Inland Revenue rules are given at the end of this chapter (see page 40).

Putting a figure on final salary pension rights

If you have worked for the same employer all your life, working out your likely pension is an easy matter. Once you have found out what fraction your scheme is based on, it is a simple matter of multiplying the number of years worked (or rather, the number of years you will have worked by the time you retire) by the fraction concerned, and then multiplying the result by your current salary.

If you are certain of promotion between now and retirement, you could bump up your salary to what you expect to be earning in your final days – but if you are anticipating only 'normal' pay rises between now and retirement then my advice is to ignore them. Normal pay rises these days – judging by national statistics – seem to be closely in line with inflation, and to plan ahead properly you really need to know the 'real' value of your likely pension, in today's purchasing power.

So, for example, if you have worked 37 years in a company whose scheme is based on one 60th, and your final salary is £40,000, your pension will be $37 \times \frac{1}{60} \times £40,000 = £24,666.66$. Or suppose you have 28 years' pensionable service in a scheme based on one 70th, and a final salary of £25,000, your pension will be $28 \times \frac{1}{70} \times £25,000 = £10,000$. Note that it is usually the number of years you have been in the company's pension scheme that counts, not the number of years you have worked for that company. They are not necessarily the same.

These figures assume that you do not take any of your pension entitlement in the form of a lump sum, although you are allowed under the rules to take up to one and a half times your final salary as tax-free cash – and most people choose to do so. (But remember: opting for the cash sum means a reduced pension.) The figures also assume that you have made no additional contributions to the scheme, which would increase the pension.

How taking cash reduces the pension
This calculation will be done for you by the scheme itself. The answer depends on a number of factors, including the age at which you retire, and whether you are a man or woman. It also depends on the generosity – or otherwise – of the particular pension scheme you belong to.

If you want a reasonable idea before you retire, you should ask your pensions department for the 'commutation factor' it uses. The answer is likely to be in the region of 9 for a man retiring at 65 and 11 for a woman retiring at 60. What you do is divide the cash sum you can expect by 9 (or 11) and the result is the amount of annual pension you will give up by taking the cash. Suppose, for instance, your expected cash is £50,000: dividing by 9 equals £5,555. Your pension will therefore be reduced by £5,555 a year. Note that, even if you do take cash, the widow's or widower's pension (payable after the member's death) is *not* usually reduced commensurately – though that depends on the scheme.

The higher the factor, the more generous your scheme is; at current interest rates, the 9 and 11 factors are actually fairly generous. Understandably, companies are not always willing to guarantee a figure if you are asking them five or more years before your retirement, but most big schemes do tend to stick with the same factors for years at a time, so the figure your company is currently using will give you a useful indication.

The effects of taking early retirement

Retiring even a few years early can have a much greater impact on your pension than you might imagine, because of the 'double whammy' effect of fewer years' worth of contributions and investment, and more years during which you will be drawing the pension. And your loss could be even greater than indicated in Table 3 if, by leaving early, you miss out on a promotion that would have increased your salary by much more than inflation.

If employers are so minded, there is often significant scope for them to improve the benefits of early retirees within the overall limits imposed by the Inland Revenue. A long-serving, valued employee who has to leave early due to ill-health, for instance, might be granted the full pension he or she would have received at the normal retirement date, although this will be based on their current earnings rather than some notional future figure.

More common – and still very generous – is the stance of companies who will allow early retirees the full value of the pension rights they have accumulated so far. Thus, someone in a one 60th scheme who had worked 20 years before retiring at age 60, say, rather than the normal 65, would be granted a pension of one third (20/60ths) of their final salary, payable from the date of his or her (early) retirement.

On a strictly 'fair' basis, such people should get less, because of the expected greater length of their retirement. Typically, the pension will be scaled down by a simple 6% for each year they retire early; retiring five years early, therefore, means a reduction in their pension of 30%. Suppose, in circumstances identical to the above, a man were entitled, before scaling down, to one third of his former salary of £30,000 – in other words, £10,000: after the scaling down, his pension will be just £7,000.

Table 3 gives some further examples of how early retirement cuts down the pension entitlement.

Table 3: The effect of early retirement in final salary pension schemes

Assuming a final salary at the date of retirement of £30,000, and a scheme which, at the normal retirement date, gives its members a pension of one 60th of final salary for each year of service.

Retiring (after) — years early	Length of service (years)	Early retirement pension	Pension at normal date	(after)	Length of service (years)
15	10	£500	£12,500		25
15	20	£1,000	£17,500		35
15	30	£1,500	£20,000		45*
10	10	£2,000	£10,000		20
10	20	£4,000	£15,000		30
10	30	£6.000	£20,000		40
5	10	£3,500	£7,500		15
5	20	£7,000	£12,500		25
5	30	£10,500	£17,500		35
3	10	£4,100	£6,500		13
3	20	£8,200	£11,500		23
3	30	£12,300	£16,500		33
1	10	£4,700	£5,500		11
1	20	£9,400	£10,500		21
1	30	£14,100	£15,300		31

*The maximum pension under Inland Revenue regulations is two-thirds final salary so 45 years' service produces no greater pension than 40 years.

(The table ignores the fact that salaries are likely to increase by inflation, but then so will most pensions, so the above is a reasonably 'fair' comparison.)

Source: Prudential

There may be some scope for negotiating with your employer if you want – or perhaps are being persuaded – to take early retirement. Big companies engaged in 'downsizing' may be reasonably generous when encouraging employees to retire early. For instance, some schemes work out the 'early' pension by crediting you with not just your actual years' service but also half the number of years between your actual retirement date and your normal retirement date. It is always worth emphasizing that the company's offer could be more generous while still obeying the

Inland Revenue maximum limits. The section at the end of the chapter gives more details on what these limits are (see page 40).

Company Money Purchase Pension Schemes

These schemes are sometimes called 'defined contribution' schemes, as opposed to the final salary-type of 'defined benefit' schemes. With money purchase schemes you know how much is going into the scheme – typically, between 6% and 8% of salary provided by the employer plus 4% by the employee. These contributions are then invested, and each year the employer's pensions department should provide its employees with a note of exactly how much his or her pension fund is worth.

There are some variations on this theme. Some schemes, for example, require a constant contribution from employees (say 4% of salary) but have different rates of employer contribution depending on your age – 5% for the under-35s, 7% for employees aged up to 50 and 10% for older staff. Again, some schemes will have just one investment fund into which all contributions are invested; other schemes might offer employees a choice of two, three or many more different types of investment fund with different degrees of risk and potential reward.

But while you can find out easily enough how much is going into your scheme each year, and the current value of your total pension savings, you do not – and cannot – know how much pension you are going to get at retirement. That depends on:

- Investment growth rates between now and the date of your retirement
- The amount of future contributions, including any additional ones made by the employee under an AVC
- Annuity rates (which in turn depend on the general level of interest rates) at the time of your retirement. Annuity rates also depend on your age at retirement and your sex: because

women live longer than men and so draw their pensions longer, annuity rates are worse for them.

Table 4 gives examples of current annuity rates at various ages. These applied when bank base rate was standing at 6.75%. The extent to which annuity rates can change is indicated in Figure 1.

Table 4: Current pension annuity rates

Amount of annual pension available for a purchase price of £10,000

	Man 65+ Wife 62*	Man 60+ Wife 57*	Man 65 —	Man 60 —	Woman 60 —
Flat pension	£976	£910	£1,114	£1,007	£933
Increasing at:					
3% a year	£755	£681	£904	£793	£708
5% a year	£606	£531	£772	£656	£565
Inflation	£605	£531	£778	£666	£568

Pension reduces to two-thirds on the first death. In all cases, payments will be made monthly in advance and are 'guaranteed' for five years – this means that if both parties die early on, payments will continue to be made to their estate for the remainder of the initial five-year period. All annuity payments – 'guaranteed' or not – will continue at the promised level as long as the annuitants live.

Source: Annuity Direct

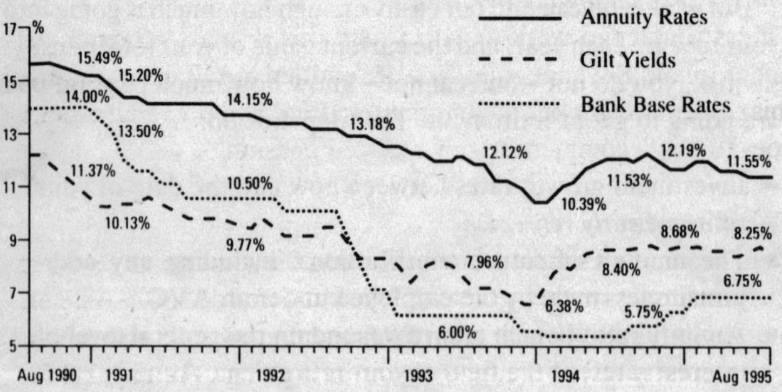

Figure 1: How annuity rates can fluctuate

People with this type of scheme are allowed to 'play the market' and take their pension fund to the company currently providing the best annuity rates available in the market on retirement. They can also decide on the frequency with which payments are made – pensions payable quarterly in arrears, for example, will be slightly higher than those paid monthly in advance.

Investment considerations

Money purchase schemes pose some particularly tricky invest-ment problems, and anyone within a few years of retirement should devote some thought to them now. The basic problem is that most money purchase pension funds are invested in equities – stocks and shares – which offer the best prospects for long-term growth, but can be volatile in the short term. But once you are within a few years of retirement, your pension savings are no longer 'long term', and you run the risk of seeing years of pension planning and saving blown off course by a collapse in the stock market just when you plan to retire.

There are various ways of grappling with this. Because the problems – and the possible solutions – are similar to those faced by people with personal pensions, they are dealt with in the following chapters (see pages 44 and 51).

The effect of taking tax-free cash

This is simpler to work out than under final salary schemes. If, under Inland Revenue rules, you are entitled to £10,000 cash, say, this comes straight out of your pension fund and the reduced sum goes to buy a commensurately reduced pension.

The effect of early retirement

Here again, it's a simple matter of getting the sums done. Retiring early means less money going into the kitty, and a shorter time for the whole fund to benefit from investment growth. It also means lower annuity rates because the pension is going to be payable for longer.

Suppose John Wilmot has built up a pension fund of £100,000 within his company's money purchase scheme when he decides to take early retirement at 60. On a salary of £30,000 he could have expected total contributions into the fund of, say, 12% of salary (£3,600) per year. By leaving five years early, he has foregone additional contributions totalling at least £18,000 (we have added in nothing for any pay rises he might have got in those years); but more important, he has forfeited the extra years of investment growth.

Had Wilmot stayed, assuming investment returns averaging 8% a year, his fund would have grown to about £170,000 – as it is, he must make do with £100,000, which will buy him a pension of about £10,000 or a little more. To make matters worse, because he is retiring younger, the annuity rate is lower. An annuity payable at age 65 is about 10% higher for any given sum than at 60; in this case the pension at age 65 would probably have been more than £19,000.

Pensions from Former Employers

Few people spend all their working lives with a single employer; most of us are likely to have bits and pieces of former pension schemes tucked away somewhere. In theory, you should hear from your old employer(s) a few months before retirement – though remember this will be the normal retirement date of that particular scheme, which may be earlier or later than the date at which you are actually planning to retire. They should provide you with full details of how much you will be getting, when, and any choices to be made – whether to take the tax-free cash, for example. If you have moved house since you left a previous employer, make sure you give them your new address now.

Most 'old' pensions of the final salary-type are not going to be very valuable, because they will not have been revalued fully (if at all) to compensate for inflation. Suppose, for example, you left a scheme in 1975 on a salary of £8,000 after 10 years' service. Assuming it was a one 60th scheme, you will receive a grand total of £1,333 a year – less if you take the tax-free cash option (see page 36).

Pension rights from former employers earned since January 1985 must be revalued annually, at inflation or 5% a year, whichever is less, but employers are not obliged to do anything about the rights accrued before that date. Only if you left a scheme after January 1991 is a full revaluation of all pension rights required – and once again this is capped at 5%.

Some big, rich, private sector schemes will opt to take a more generous stance on pre-1985 rights. Former civil servants and other government workers definitely have the advantage here: generally speaking, all their preserved rights are revalued fully in line with inflation, and have been for a long time.

There is one exception to these general rules. Under a 'contracted-out' final salary scheme – one which opted out of the State Earnings Related Pension Scheme (Serps) by promising to pay its members at least as much as Serps would have provided – that portion of preserved pension rights (known as the 'guaranteed minimum pension') must be fully revalued in line with national average earnings, ever since Serps began in 1978.

The outlook is brighter where your old employer ran a money purchase-type pension scheme: the money invested in the pension fund on your behalf should simply have carried on growing after you left – and, assuming reasonable investment performance, should more than compensate for inflation since you left.

Tracing old pension schemes

Problems can arise where people have lost touch with former employers – particularly if that company has since been taken over – but the state-run Pensions Schemes Registry may be able to help. The Registry was set up in 1991 and currently has details of nearly 200,000 different pension schemes (past and present). The service, which is free, currently scores an 86% success rate and the process usually takes 'two or three days'. Contact the agency and ask for form PR4 (see Appendix I, page 161).

Problems with old pension schemes

The Registry can only supply information, it cannot help with any problems that might arise concerning the pension. If you have a query, contact the Occupational Pensions Advisory Service (OPAS) – another free service, this time run on a voluntary basis. OPAS can be contacted either via Citizen's Advice Bureaux, or through its head office (see Appendix I, page 161).

OPAS is the first port of call for anyone with a problem concerning a company pension. But if they cannot sort the matter out, contact the Pensions Ombudsman (see Appendix I, page 161), who deals primarily with occupational pension schemes (for problems with personal pensions, see Chapter 5, page 66). The scheme, which is a statutory one, was set up a few years ago to deal with complaints arising in two areas: first, complaints of injustice arising from maladministration by the trustees or managers of a pension scheme; and secondly, disputes of fact or law concerning pension schemes. Injustice includes distress, delay or inconvenience.

The Pensions Ombudsman cannot act on matters relating to State pensions, or to armed forces pensions where the individual is a serving member of the scheme, or on disputes of fact or law relating to most public service pensions. Nor can he act on matters which are already subject to court proceedings. Finally, there is a time limit of three years within which a complaint must be made. Decisions by the Ombudsman are binding to both parties, subject only to an appeal on a point of law to the High Court or the Court of Sessions in Scotland. For further details of the scheme, there is a free booklet, *The Pensions Ombudsman – How He Can Help You*.

The Tax-free Lump Sum: Should You Take It?

With the vast majority of company pension schemes employees are entitled to take a tax-free lump sum of up to one and a half times their final salary, depending on their length of service and when they joined the scheme. Taking the cash, as we have seen, cuts down the pension, so should you take this option or not? Most people do take it, and often spend part of it on the 'holiday of a lifetime', marking the start of a whole new phase of life.

Perhaps you have done your sums and realize that your retirement income is going to be fairly stretched: should you then forgo the lump sum and take the higher pension? There are plenty of reasons why you might still want to take the cash: it will be more flexible, and you will be able to leave something to your heirs (remember, the pension dies with you – or your widow or widower).

But even if income is your prime consideration, it may well be a good idea to take the cash and use it to buy an ordinary annuity instead. These are taxed less heavily than pension annuities, so the net result, after tax, can leave you with more disposable income, as the following example shows.

John Keats, who is unmarried, retires at 65 after 40 years' service on a salary of £30,000, which gives him a pension of £20,000 a year. He could take a lump sum of £45,000 (one and a half times final salary) plus a reduced pension of £15,000 a year (using the commutation factor of 9, as described on page 28). His choices are therefore:

- **Full pension:** *£20,000 a year, increasing in line with inflation (or 5% a year, whichever is less)*
- **Reduced pension:** *£15,000 a year, increasing in line with inflation, plus £45,000 lump sum.*

Investing the £45,000 in an ordinary annuity provides Keats with an income of £4,860 a year gross. However, because of its tax advantages, his net income after basic-rate tax would be £4,400 from the annuity, while his net income from the top £5,000 slice of his full pension would only amount to £3,750. In terms of his immediate income, therefore, Keats would be better off taking the cash and investing it in an ordinary annuity. However, he should remember that this annuity will not increase in line with inflation, unlike his company pension.

In fact, after reading the rest of this book and consulting a financial adviser, he decides on a third course of action: to take the cash, use £33,000 to buy an ordinary annuity, and the remainder to feed into a Corporate Bond Pep for the next couple of years (£6,000 a year). This will give him a return of 8% a year on the cash invested and, more importantly, the income will be completely free of tax. He realizes that the capital value of such Peps is likely to fluctuate, but as he says, with annuities you say goodbye to all the capital for ever, so a little fluctuation in an investment isn't going to concern him.

His post-retirement income is therefore going to look like this:

	Gross	Net
Annual pension	£15,000	£11,250*
Income from ordinary annuity	£3,564	£3,227
Income from Bond Pep	£960	£960
Total		**£15,437**
Compared to:		
Full pension	£20,000	**£15,000***
or:		
Reduced pension	£15,000	£11,250*
Income from ordinary annuity	£4,860	£4,400
Total	£19,860	**£15,650**

*It has been assumed that the full pension is taxable at basic rate.

- **Benefits of his choice:** *he retains the £12,000 capital sum to leave to his heirs and at the same time actually increases his immediate, after-tax income.*
- **Drawback:** *only the first slice of his income (the pension) will increase in line with inflation.*

The above example is based on a final salary scheme. The same principles apply to a company money purchase scheme, but because these work very much like personal pensions, an example is shown in Chapter 5 (see page 66).

General points to note

Taking the lump sum to invest in an ordinary annuity will usually provide a better after-tax income, but unfortunately it is impossible to be categoric: every individual must do his or her own homework first. The answer will depend on:

- **The rate obtained for the ordinary annuity.** They differ from company to company: consult a broker to obtain the best rates. You are likely to find that ordinary annuity rates are slightly lower than pension annuity rates (with good reason – because nobody is forced to buy one, they are favoured by those people in good health and with a long life expectancy – thus making the business a 'worse bet' for the company that sells them).

- **Your tax position.** The tax advantages of the ordinary annuity over the pension annuity are greatest if you are a higher-rate taxpayer, less but still considerable if you are a basic-rate taxpayer, and irrelevant if you are a non-taxpayer.

- **Your age and sex.** The way that ordinary annuity payments are taxed is as follows. The Inland Revenue decrees that a certain proportion of each annuity payment should be defined as 'capital content' – in effect, a partial return of your own capital – and this sum is tax-free; only the balance is taxable. Since the 1995 budget, the taxable element is taxed at a rate of only 20%, and basic-rate taxpayers have no further liability. Higher rate taxpayers will, however, have to pay an extra 20% tax on top. The size of the capital content depends on your age at purchase, as shown below.

Ordinary annuities: amount of tax-free capital content per year on payments produced by a £10,000 purchase price

Man aged 60	£466	Woman aged 60	£398
Man aged 65	£570	Woman aged 65	£482
Man aged 70	£712	Woman aged 70	£600

Note: this assumes the annuity is payable monthly in arrears and is without a guaranteed period.

Source: Inland Revenue

One gambit to consider, especially for those retiring early, is taking the cash, and 'parking' it for a few years in, for example, a building society account or perhaps partly in a Corporate Bond Pep. You can then buy an ordinary annuity in a few years' time: your age then will qualify you for both higher annuity rates and a higher tax-free capital content.

Inland Revenue Rules on Company Pension Schemes

Pension schemes are some of the most tax-favoured of all investments. The pension funds themselves are almost entirely free of both income tax and capital gains tax, while contributions into the scheme attract full income tax relief. The only drawback is that the pension itself, once it starts being paid, is taxed as ordinary earned income. Not surprisingly, these tax freedoms are accompanied by rules imposing maximum limits on sums that can be saved in and withdrawn from pension schemes. Various references have been made throughout this chapter to these maximum limits, and fuller details appear below.

The rules allow for much higher pensions than most people are likely to receive, but some individuals may run up against the rules, particularly if they are taking early retirement. Set out below is a reasonably complete run-down of the rules, but pensions legislation is *extremely* complicated, so you should take this as a guide only.

Limits on contributions
Earnings cap: Anyone who joined their pension scheme after 1 June 1989 (or a new scheme set up after 14 March 1989) is subject to the overall earnings cap. This generally increases each year in line with the Retail Price Index: for the tax year 1995–96 the figure is £78,600; for the tax year 1996–97 it is £82,200. The cap affects all aspects of the pensions rules, as regards both contributions and benefits. Employees who joined their scheme before the relevant dates are not affected.

Employer's contributions: There are no specific limits on employer's contributions. However, there are rules to prevent a company 'overfunding' for the maximum pension allowable.

Employees' contributions: Employees may save a total of 15% of their taxable remuneration each year into a pension. Contributions to an Additional Voluntary Contribution (AVC) scheme are added to those made into the main scheme.

'Taxable remuneration' includes the taxable value of everything employees receive from their employer, including, for example, company cars, private medical insurance and occasional bonuses. It may be considerably more than your salary. There is, however, an overall limit of £11,790 (15% of £78,600) for the tax year 1995–96 for employees subject to the earnings cap. For 1995–96 the overall limit is £12,330 (15% of £82,200).

Limits on benefits
The pension: The maximum pension payable is two-thirds of final salary, provided the employee has clocked up sufficient years of service with the employer. A maximum of one and a half times salary can be taken as a tax-free cash sum, although this reduces the pension. In addition there can be a widow's or widower's pension of two-thirds the maximum pension (even if the employee chooses the cash sum plus reduced pension), and the whole lot can increase by 3% a year or inflation, whichever is the greater. The pension scheme can also provide up to four times salary on death before retirement.

Length of service required to achieve maximum pension: This depends on when you joined the scheme; details are given in Table 5. People who have a fluctuating income can to some extent choose which of their most recent pre-retirement years to use as an indicator of 'final salary'. These rules are more strict for controlling directors than for ordinary employees.

Table 5: Length of service requirements

Years of service to normal retirement age	MAXIMUM PENSION AS FRACTION OF FINAL SALARY	
	Joined before 17 March 1987	*Joined after 17 March 1987*
1	1/60th	2/60ths
2	2/60ths	4/60ths
3	3/60ths	6/60ths
4	4/60ths	8/60ths
5	5/60ths	10/60ths
6	8/60ths	12/60ths
7	16/60ths	14/60ths
8	24/60ths	16/60ths
9	32/60ths	18/60ths
10	40/60ths	20/60ths
11–20	40/60ths	increasing by 2/60ths a year up to a maximum 40/60ths after 20 years

These rules apply whether you have a final salary or money purchase occupational scheme. With the latter, if investment performance has been exceptionally good, the amount in the fund may buy a pension greater than these limits (though this is an exceedingly rare problem). If this is the case, the Inland Revenue steps in to prevent it.

The cash sum: The basic rule is that up to one and a half times final salary may be taken as a tax-free cash sum. This requires a certain length of service, depending on when you joined the scheme.

- **Member before March 1987:** the maximum can be obtained after 20 years' service, if the pension scheme's rules itself allow this.
- **Joined between March 1987 and June 1989:** the maximum

can be obtained after 20 years' service, but there is an overriding cash limit of £150,000.

- **Joined after June 1989:** either 2.25 times the pension, or 3/80ths of final salary for each year of service, whichever is the greater. 'Final salary' in this case is capped at £78,600 (1995–96) and £82,200 (1996–97).

4 ‖ *Saving Extra for Your Pension*

People who can anticipate retiring on a full two-thirds pension are few and far between – perhaps 1% of the entire population. So even for those who are not contemplating early retirement, there is a lot to be said for making a last-minute push on savings to increase post-retirement income.

As with all financial planning, there are various ways to achieve this: depending on your circumstances and attitudes, you may choose to put any spare money into Personal Equity Plans (Peps), a Tax-Exempt Special Savings Account (Tessa), or use your company's Additional Voluntary Contribution scheme (AVCs).

The earlier you can start this extra saving the better. Over a longer period you will obviously be able to build up greater sums, but you will also be able to afford to take greater risks and thus, in all likelihood, benefit from greater returns. Over the long term equities (i.e. company shares), have always proved to be very rewarding investments, but there is a downside: stock markets can, and do, go down as well as up. If you have less than two or three years to go before retirement, the risk of investing on the stock market is fairly high. It may fall just when you retire and cannot afford to wait for it to recover (which, over time, it always has done).

So for those within two to three years of retirement, the most appropriate investment is likely to be a low-risk deposit or fixed interest fund, and it is possible in most cases to invest in such a fund via an AVC scheme.

AVCs: the Rules

All employees are allowed to save up to 15% of their salary each year in a company pension scheme. For the purposes of the Inland

Revenue, 'salary' is defined as all the taxable benefits an employee receives from his or her job, so it can include, for instance, extra money paid for overtime, the taxable value of a company car, and so on. While most company schemes demand a contribution from their employees expressed as a percentage of their salary (usually between 4 and 8%), companies generally interpret salary as 'basic pay' (at most). Many companies actually reduce this 'basic' by around £3,000 a year, on the basis that the State pension fully covers this first slice of earnings.

So an employee paying 4% into the company's main pension scheme will have scope for putting at least a further 11% of his or her basic pay into an AVC, and possibly quite a bit more, especially after all the taxable 'extras' are taken into account.

Remember, however, that the Revenue also imposes limits at the other end on the size of pension and cash sum available, depending on the number of years worked. Occasionally people may find that they have 'overfunded' their pension, although this is highly unlikely unless you are taking very early retirement. As Table 5 (see page 42) shows, people who have worked less than 20 years for their employer by the time they retire may be limited to a lower proportion of salary as pension. In these circumstances the taxman will return any excess, less a tax charge at the special rate of 35%. Higher-rate taxpayers will then have to hand over a further 15% of the balance. So, clearly, whoever runs your AVC scheme has to take care that you do not get caught in this trap.

There are yet further Revenue rules on how the benefits from an AVC fund may be taken, which differ according to when you joined your company scheme and started making AVC payments:

- **Before April 1987:** Benefits from an AVC fund may be taken either as cash (within the overall limits of one and a half times final salary, depending on length of service) or as additional pension.
- **After 8 April 1987 and before 14 March 1989:** Benefits from an AVC fund must be taken as pension – so any cash

entitlement must come from the benefits arising under the main company scheme. The only exceptions are where the total pension (main scheme plus AVC) is deemed 'trivial' (less than £260 a year), in which case cash (less a 20% tax charge) can be taken, or where the individual suffers from serious ill-health.

- **After 14 March 1989:** For schemes set up after this date, or for people who joined existing schemes after 1 June 1989, the restriction is the same as in April 1987–March 1989, but with the additional constraint of the 'earnings cap', which limits the maximum final salary that can be taken into account (see page 40). However, such schemes allow the cash entitlement to be 2.25 times the full starting pension (including the AVC portion) and so boosts the available cash.

Types of AVC scheme

Since the late 1980s companies which run pension schemes have been obliged by law to offer their members an 'in-house' AVC scheme. As a general rule these are likely to have lower charges than the alternative, 'free-standing' AVC scheme (or FSAVC), which are individual plans sold by life assurance companies. However, the free-standing versions may offer a wider investment choice.

Nearly all AVCs (in-house or free-standing) work in the same way as a money purchase pension scheme: they build up an invested fund for the individual which must then be used in the prescribed way at retirement. However, a few big company schemes of the final salary-type still offer their members an AVC scheme based on 'added years', where the money saved goes towards buying extra years' service for the purpose of deciding the fraction of salary a member is entitled to on retirement. These are likely to offer the best value of all, especially for those close to retirement.

AVCs and tax relief

Like all qualifying pension savings, contributions to an AVC are tax-deductible. With an in-house scheme the amount is knocked off your gross pay before tax is levied, so you get 'instant' relief, no matter what your tax rate is. With an FSAVC you pay the pension premium net of basic-rate tax (which the life company must then claim back from the Revenue on your behalf). If you are a higher-rate taxpayer, you get the balance of the tax relief through your annual tax assessment.

The other major tax 'perk' which applies to all qualifying pension savings is that the invested funds are substantially free from both income tax and capital gains tax. This means, all other things being equal, that the fund should grow faster than a taxed fund; as a rough-and-ready figure, if a taxed fund were to grow by 7.5% a year, an equivalent untaxed fund would grow by 9%.

AVCs in practice
The whole point of saving through an AVC is to increase post-retirement income. But exactly how much pension the AVC fund will buy depends on what pension annuity rates are at the time of retirement. The example below shows one scenario.

William Wordsworth retires on his 65th birthday from Lakeland Products plc in January 1996, after 28 years' pensionable service and on a final salary of £30,000. His wife Dorothy is three years younger than him. Lakeland Products' company pension scheme is a 1/60th final salary scheme with a widow's pension of two-thirds the full pension. He has also, in the last few years, been contributing regularly to an AVC scheme and has built up a fund of £16,000. His options are as follows:

1. Taking the whole amount as pension
Pension from main scheme
$^{28}/_{60} \times £30,000$ £14,000
(reducing to £9,333 after his death, payable to his widow)

plus

Pension from AVC*   £1,511
(reducing to £1,007 after his death, payable to his widow)

Total pension   **£15,511**

2. Taking tax-free cash

Maximum tax-free cash	£45,000
Reduced main pension	£9,000
plus	
AVC pension*	£1,511
Total pension	**£10,511**

Note: William will also be entitled to the basic State pension, plus graduated pension of £4.50 a week from an earlier employment. This adds a further £5,145 a year to his annual income. However, he has no entitlement to any earnings-related addition, nor does he have any pension due from earlier employments.

*The size of the AVC pension depends on annuity rates at retirement.
Source: Annuity Direct

Last-minute savings with AVCs

Even if you are only a few years away from retirement, it can be worthwhile making contributions to an AVC scheme. Suppose you have just three years to go before retirement, and wish to increase your pension. The following example shows how this might be achieved:

Bill Langland is 57 and will be retiring in three years' time at age 60. He has a company pension scheme which will provide a pension at retirement of 20/60ths his final salary, currently £30,000. The scheme is non-contributory.

He decides to save the maximum possible in an AVC scheme to increase his pension.

Expected pension from work		£10,000
AVC saving: 15% of £30,000	£4,500	
Total invested over 3 years	£13,500	
Total net cost (after tax relief at 40%)	£8,100	
Value of AVC fund at retirement	£15,479	
Additional pension available		£1,400
Total pension		**£11,400**

This table assumes, for convenience, that his salary will not increase between now and retirement. It also assumes the AVC fund will earn 7% a year while it is invested. This might seem on the low side, but it would be sensible, with only three years to go, to steer clear of the riskier (if potentially more rewarding) stock market-based funds and opt for a building society or fixed interest based fund, in which case the return is realistic.

The pension figure assumes Langland is married, that his wife is three years younger than himself, and that the pension will reduce by one third on the first death. It is based on annuity rates currently available. A single man aged 60 could buy a pension of approximately £1,550 a year with the same sum.

In the above example income tax relief was available at 40% on the full AVC saving, and if the saver is then only liable to basic-rate tax after retirement, he or she will have done especially well, achieving a net income for life (in the above example) of £1,050 in return for a total capital outlay of £8,100. Where savers do not experience this drop in tax rates, the figures look less impressive. The total cost to a basic-rate taxpayer of making similar AVC contributions would be £10,260 rather than £8,100. This makes the AVC less attractive, but in most cases still worth doing.

AVCs or Peps?

The above example assumes that the saver is caught by the post-1987 rules, in which case the accumulated fund must be turned into pension. People whose scheme membership pre-dates that are allowed to take their cash out of their AVC fund instead, and for such people, especially the higher-rate taxpayers, the AVC is an investment bargain.

If you cannot take the cash, you might consider using a Personal Equity Plan (Pep) as a home for last-minute retirement savings rather than the AVC. Peps are dealt with more fully in Chapters 9 and 10 (see pages 98 and 107), but the basic principle is that funds are tax-free, and income can be withdrawn from them on a tax-free basis. However, there is no income tax relief on money going into a Pep, unlike the AVC.

Which vehicle you choose will depend on personal circumstances and there is no 'right' answer except, perhaps, to do both. But if your income – or the desire to save it – does not stretch that far, then go for the Pep if you want access to a capital sum more than the provision of extra income. However, anyone who expects their marginal tax rate to fall after retirement will probably do better with the AVC.

The Open Market Option

Finally, it should be noted that you do not have to buy the pension annuity from the organization with whom you saved the AVC funds; you can take it to any other pension-providing company in the marketpace at that time, which is known as exercising the 'open market option'. It would be wise at least to check out this opportunity, because it may well lead to an improved pension.

There are a number of choices to be made when buying an annuity. As these are identical to those facing people with personal pensions, the topic is dealt with in the following chapter.

5 | *Personal and Self-employed Pensions*

Personal pension plans and their predecessors, the retirement annuity plans (RAPs), are the vehicles which are used by those who have not been able to join an occupational scheme – either because they are self-employed or because their employer does not run a company scheme.

If you have been in this situation for a while, you may well have several plans of both types with a number of different insurance companies. Whether you have a PPP or an RAP, there are no Revenue limits on the amount that can be built up in the pension funds (or the pension it eventually produces), but there are limits on the amounts that can be put in, expressed as a percentage of 'net relevant earnings' – broadly defined as 'taxable earned income' for employees and 'taxable profit' for the self-employed. The limits increase progressively with age, so most people, for most of their working lives, never actually reach those limits.

In the last few vital years before retirement, however, you may be getting close to those limits. In some cases people need to plan carefully whether to add to their personal pension or their RAP because the Revenue limits operate in slightly different ways. As Table 6 shows, both impose a maximum percentage of earnings that can be saved in a pension plan, but the personal pension has an additional limitation in that maximum earnings are subject to the earnings cap (£78,600 for 1995–96 and £82,200 for 1996–97). This means that high earners may be able to save more via their RAP, despite the percentage limits being lower. (Note that RAPs are no longer available for new entrants, but anyone with an existing scheme may continue to add to it.)

Table 6: Maximum contributions to personal pensions and RAPs expressed as percentage of net relevant earnings

Age on 6 April	Personal pension	RAP	RAP premiums higher for earnings over:	
			1995–96	1996–97
Up to 36	17.5%	17.5%	£78,600	£82,200
36–45	20.0%	17.5%	£89,829	£93,943
46–50	25.0%	17.5%	£112,236	£117,429
51–55	30.0%	20.0%	£117,900	£123,300
56–60	35.0%	22.5%	£122,267	£127,857
61–74	40.0%	27.5%	£114,327	£119,563

Note: in all cases up to 5% of net relevant earnings may be extracted from the maximum and used to buy life assurance cover.

Source: Taxbriefs

Tax Reliefs

Both RAPs and personal pensions qualify for tax relief on premiums at the individual's highest rate of income tax. The self-employed pay the premiums gross and the tax relief is given through the annual tax return. Employees paying into RAPs pay gross too and get their relief through the tax coding, but with personal pensions they pay the premiums net of basic-rate tax; higher-rate taxpayers have the appropriate adjustment made through their coding each year.

The pension funds, in both cases, are substantially free from income tax and capital gains tax. At retirement (generally allowed from age 50 under a personal pension, and from age 60 under a RAP) the bulk of the fund must be used to buy a pension annuity, which is taxed as earned income.

However, a proportion can be taken as a tax-free lump sum: under personal pension rules, 25% of the total fund can be taken as cash; under RAP rules, the maximum cash is three times the remaining annual pension. In practice, the RAP formula usually produces a cash sum of between 25% and 35% of the fund – with the higher percentage generally available to those retiring later (the older you are when you buy a pension annuity, the higher the level). With both types of plan a pension must be taken by the age of 75.

Under the 'carry back' provisions, people are allowed to backtrack over their six previous years' earnings to pay in the appropriate percentages of income to their plan – this is particularly useful to the self-employed, whose income might fluctuate significantly from year to year. A separate set of provisions, known as the 'carry forward' rules, enables savers to choose which of two years' earnings certain premiums may be set against.

Countdown to Retirement: Investment Risk and Income

Note: *this section should also be read by anyone with a company money purchase-type scheme, or an AVC scheme which must be turned into an annuity, as many of the considerations involved and the choices outlined are also available to them.*

Once you are within a few years of retirement, you should start to have an idea of how much your pension savings are likely to produce in the way of retirement income. Even within a year or so of the big day this can only be an educated guess – and that applies whether the guess comes from you or the insurance company which runs the scheme and will supply 'estimates' on request. This is because annuity rates change from time to time, while investment conditions may increase (or reduce!) the value of the funds invested.

Nevertheless, it is a good idea to carry out a 'stock-taking' exercise, say five years before retirement, and increase your pension savings if serious shortcomings are revealed.

There is another reason why you should start thinking about the end result a few years before retirement. The very way these individual pensions work gives rise to some tricky investment problems. During perhaps 20 to 30 years of your working life, you are salting away pension premiums (usually invested in equities) in preparation for a single day – your retirement day – when the whole fund is suddenly converted into cash and buys the annuity for you to live on for the rest of your life.

But what if you had the bad luck to retire on the day of a stock market crash – or on a day when pension annuity rates fell in the wake of a tumble in interest rates? In either case, years of careful planning could be thrown into disarray and by then, of course, it is too late for you to do anything about it – unless you can delay retiring, which is not always possible.

Fortunately, there are a number of ways in which this investment risk can be tackled, but some require careful advance planning. There are, broadly speaking, two ways to diminish this risk. The first is to change the underlying investments in your pension fund gradually as the big day approaches, moving away from (more volatile) equities and progressively into the more stable environment of fixed interest or cash funds. Most pension plans allow such 'switching' between different funds, often at either a very low, or no cost. This approach is best carried out gradually over, say, five years, switching 20% of the total fund each year. You may lose out on a few years' worth of the superior investment growth provided by equities, but your pension savings will be less vulnerable overall to swings in the stock market.

The alternative is to tackle the problem from the other end, so to speak. This can be achieved in a number of ways:

- by choosing a pension annuity which is linked to equities rather than fixed interest
- by 'staggering' your retirement so that you do not cash in all your pension policies on the same day, but gradually, over a period of years
- by operating a new scheme known as an 'income withdrawal scheme' or 'drawdown scheme' whereby, instead of converting your pension fund into an annuity, you make withdrawals directly from the fund to provide a retirement income.

You will probably need professional advice to help you to decide which, if any, of these routes might suit you, but make sure that you understand the broad principles of each – and how exactly such advice can help – before you decide.

All the choices outlined below are open to those with personal pensions or RAPs. Those in a final salary scheme who have built up an AVC fund can choose between options 1 and 2 below. Those with a company money purchase scheme can choose options 3 or 4 by 'converting' their scheme, just before retirement, into a personal pension. Professional advice at this stage is essential.

1 Traditional, fixed interest annuities

Despite their problems, traditional annuities have two advantages over the alternatives: they produce the highest immediate income available for any given capital sum and, once in payment, are guaranteed to last at that level for the rest of the pensioner's (or spouse's) life, however long that may be.

All personal pensions, and most RAPs, allow policyholders to take their accumulated pension funds at retirement and place them with the provider offering the highest annuity rates at that time. This is known as exercising the 'open market option' and it is usually well worth doing. Annuity payments can vary by 5 or 10% from company to company, and those which are the best investment managers are rarely the best annuity providers. There are a number of independent financial advisers who specialize in this area.

Annuities come in various shapes and sizes, and the amount of income they pay depends on, first and foremost, the level of interest rates at the time the annuity is taken; and on the age (and sex) of the individual at the time he or she buys the annuity (the older the policyholder, the higher the income will be; women, living longer than men on average, can expect a smaller income).

There are a number of variations on this type of annuity which will affect the amount of immediate income a given capital sum will buy. These are as follows:

- **Fixed or increasing income.** The highest immediate income is available from a fixed annuity, which pays the same amount per year during the annuitant's life. Other options are annuities which increase at a fixed rate of 3%, 4% or 5% a year, or by an amount linked to the Retail Prices Index.
- **Frequency of payment.** Payments can be made monthly in advance or quarterly or even annually in arrears. The longer the delay, the higher the payments will be.
- **Joint life or single life.** Annuity payments can last for the annuitant's life only or, if married, until the second death.
- **Level of widow's (or widower's) pension.** After the first death, payments under joint life pension annuities can continue at either 50%, two-thirds, or 100% of the previous level.
- **Guaranteed period.** Annuity payments last for life – but if you (and your spouse) died the day after taking one out, no capital would be returned to your estates. It is possible to obtain partial protection against this loss by opting for a 'guaranteed' period (typically, five or 10 years), during which payments will continue to be paid out, even if both partners have died.

Table 7 gives some typical examples of annuity rates that were available in October 1995, according to these different circumstances.

If you are comparing quotes with the one provided by your existing pension company, it is clearly vital to ensure the conditions are identical as regards the frequency of payment, whether fixed or escalating, and the level of widow(er)'s pension – otherwise you may be misled into thinking that one offer is better than another when it is not.

Table 7: Typical annuity rates for a capital sum of £10,000

	Single man aged 65				Single woman aged 60		
Income	*No guarantee*	*Guaranteed*		*Income*	*No guarantee*	*Guaranteed*	
		5 years	*10 years*			*5 years*	*10 years*
Level	£1,137	£1,114	£1,043	Level	£938	£933	£917
3%	£921	£904	£870	3%	£712	£708	£678
5%	£788	£772	£732	5%	£567	£565	£552
RPI	£810	£778	£738	RPI	£576	£568	£562

Joint lives, man aged 65, wife aged 62; payments guaranteed for 5 years

Income	*Level of spouse's pension after first death*		
	50%	*67%*	*100%*
Level	£1,007	£976	£919
3%	£787	£755	£698
5%	£638	£606	£551
RPI	£640	£605	£544

All payments in these examples will be made monthly in advance.

Source: Annuity Direct

How to choose between the different fixed rate types of annuity: There are no general guidelines here; much will depend on your own circumstances. The following points might be worth bearing in mind:

- Opting for payments made quarterly in arrears rather than months in advance will result in an increase in annual income of perhaps 1.5 or 2%.
- Delaying taking the pension on average increases income by around 2% for each year of delay.
- If you chose a pension increasing at 3% a year, it will take around six years before that pension overtakes the amount paid on a level-income annuity; with a 5% annual increase, it takes between seven and eight years.
- The RPI-linked annuities depend in part on the market's

perception of the outlook for inflation; it if looks as if inflation is set to rise, RPI-linked annuities will offer much lower starting rates.

- If you are married, it is probably wisest to opt for a pension which includes a widow's or widower's pension, so that it continues to be paid (usually at a lower rate) after the planholder's death. However, this involves a lower pension overall, as the above table indicates, and your decision here must depend on personal circumstances. For example, if your partner is a lot older than you, he or she is likely to predecease you, in which case that portion of the pension will be 'wasted'.

- Married couples who both have good pensions in their own right should remember that, if both partners buy a pension with widow(er)'s rights attached, then one – by definition – will be 'wasted'. Buying a single life annuity is likely to give you a higher income.

- Those who suffer from ill-health – and habitual smokers – may be able to get better rates than these, because their life expectancy is diminished. Professional financial advice should be sought in these circumstances.

How changing interest rates affect annuity payments: Annuity rates depend on the general level of interest rates at the date of purchase. The extent to which they may change is shown by Figure 1 (see page 32). But while this shows the change in the underlying rate, it may be more useful to see the effect this has on specific situations. As a rule of thumb, if the underlying interest rate falls or rises by 1%, annuity income will fall (or rise) by around 5%.

2 With-profit and unit-linked annuities

With these annuities, the amount paid out depends partly on the level of interest rates and partly on the performance of an under-lying investment fund. If the investment performs well, then payments under the annuity should rise over the years, but there is some investment risk.

At the outset, the annuitant specifies a level of income that he or she wants from the annuity, which requires that investment growth should reach a target level during that year. Assuming it succeeds, they will get the income specified; if not, the income paid out will be less, so such annuities are not suitable for people operating on extremely tight budgets.

Buyers can help themselves by choosing a reasonably modest starting income which does not anticipate too much future growth. And in the past, at any rate, these annuities have proved to be a rewarding choice. Table 8 below shows some actual examples of how such annuities – with various levels of 'anticipated' future growth – have performed in the past, while Table 9 outlines the range of choices for someone buying such an annuity today. Unit-linked and with-profits annuities basically do the same job, but their approach is slightly different: the with-profits option is the lower risk approach.

Table 8: Past performance of with-profits annuities

Annuity taken out by couple aged 60 in 1987. Purchase price: £100,000. Widow/er's pension: 100% of joint pension.

Year	*With-profits annuity* Annual growth rate anticipated:			*Fixed rate annuity*
	3.5%	*6.0875%*	*8.1575%*	*n.a.*
1987	£5,857	£7,550	£8,992	£10,128
1988	£6,318	£7,945	£9,282	£10,128
1989	£7,251	£8,897	£10,195	£10,128
1990	£8,407	£10,063	£11,310	£10,128
1991	£9,031	£10,547	£11,627	£10,128
1992	£9,752	£11,111	£12,014	£10,128
1993	£10,384	£11,542	£12,242	£10,128
1994	£11,337	£12,294	£12,790	£10,128
1995	£12,049	£12,748	£13,008	£10,128

Table 9: Unit-linked annuities – the choice on purchase

Amount of annual income paid in return for a capital sum of £10,000.
Single man aged 65.

	Assumed rate of growth	Starting income	Income after 10 years of actual annual growth of:		
			6%	9%	12%
1.	8% p.a.	£936	£738	£976	£1,280
2.	4% p.a.	£692	£796	£1,050	£1,380
3.	0% p.a.	£470	£799	£1,050	£1,380

Note: the equivalent fixed rate annuity for a single man aged 65 would be £936 for the same £10,000.

After 20 years of 9% growth, option 1 would be paying out £1,010 p.a., option 2 £1,600 and option 3 £2,380.

Source: Equitable Life

There are two respects in which these annuities are a lot less risky than conventional ones: the level of income does not depend entirely on where interest rates happen to be on the day of your retirement; and you do not have to make the big jump with your pension fund, out of equities and into fixed interest, on one particular day – your fund is effectively staying within the realms of equities – so a stock market crash will not affect your income in the same way.

Most company money purchase schemes will allow their members to buy such annuities, but because of the company pension rules, which limit the maximum pension payable by reference to final salary, you can buy one only from a company which undertakes to monitor, for the Inland Revenue, the amount of pension paid each year to ensure it does not overstep those limits.

These annuities might well suit those who have built up in their company scheme an AVC fund which they must turn into an annuity. Because most of their pension will be coming from the company's main scheme, they can probably afford to take a little more risk with the AVC portion. Those retiring young, who are in particular need of some sort of inflation-proofing in their income, might also opt for with-profits or unit-linked annuities.

Over the long term, such an equity-linked investment should always outperform the fixed interest securities on which a conventional annuity is based, but if stock market growth does not match the rate assumed, the income will inevitably fall. So it is best to opt for the lowest growth rate you can afford (bearing in mind that the lower the rate assumed, the lower the immediate income).

Mixing annuities: With most pension schemes you do not have to buy a single annuity, although if your total pension fund is not that large, you may come up against minimum investment requirements. Suppose, however, you have a total pension fund worth £100,000 on retirement: you could split this and have half in a conventional annuity and half in a with-profits or unit-linked one.

3 Phased retirement and staggered vesting

These are two popular catch-phrases in the pensions industry at present. They both refer to something that self-employed people in particular have been doing in an informal way for years. Instead of turning all their pension policies into annuities in one go, they have 'phased' them in over a period of years, as they gradually wind down from work. As their working income winds down, they can gradually build up their pension income.

This, of course, assumes that people have more than one policy; these days, companies generally 'segment' their pensions policies into hundreds of small parts. This segmentation is notional in a sense, as it makes no difference to the way the policy is invested or run; its purpose is purely to allow such phasing to take place. As long as people obey the overall age limits on retirement – between 50 and 75, with a personal pension – they can phase them in at any time. And because annuity rates rise the older you are when you make the purchase, the delay is likely to mean extra pension as well. Note, however, that if interest rates in general fall during your years of retirement, the amount of annuity each segment purchases could also fall as the drop in interest rates may outweigh the factor of increasing age.

This informal 'phasing' has now been taken a step further with the concept called 'staggered vesting'. This requires pensions policies to be segmented into 100 or more parts, and the idea is that each year a certain number of these parts are encashed to provide that year's income, leaving the rest invested to benefit from future growth. The scheme makes use of the 25% tax-free cash entitlement from each policy to produce the first slice of each year's income. Table 10 shows how it could work in practice.

Table 10: Staggered vesting in practice

Pension fund: £300,000. Target yearly income: £20,000. Tax rate: 25%

Age	Starting fund	Amount encashed	Tax-free + cash	Annuity = payment	Total income	Remaining fund
60	£294,000*	£66,000	£16,500	£3,510	£20,010	£228,000
61	£248,000	£53,700	£13,400	£6,550	£19,950	£194,000
62	£210,000	£43,700	£10,900	£9,060	£19,960	£167,000
63	£181,000	£35,400	£8,850	£11,100	£19,950	£145,000
64	£158,000	£28,500	£7,140	£12,800	£19,940	£129,000

and so on until . . .

Age	Starting fund	Amount encashed	Tax-free + cash	Annuity = payment	Total income	Remaining fund
73	£118,000	£3,360	£840	£19,100	£19,940	£114,000
74	£124,000	£2,580	£645	£19,300	£19,945	£121,000
75	£132,000**					

*Note that there is an initial charge on the scheme which immediately knocks down the £300,000 to £294,000.

**This will provide: tax-free cash of £33,000 plus an additional pension of £10,200 p.a., alongside the continuing pension of £19,300.

The table assumes level annuity payments and annual growth on investments remaining within the fund of 9%. If they grew by lesser amounts, the pension income would diminish with age. Remember that each year's annuity payments are added to those being made from annuities taken out in earlier years. All payments are shown net of 25% tax.

Note that the way this particular scheme has been constructed gives rise to a big leap in income from age 75. It would be possible, by cashing in more segments in the earlier years, to have a smoother progression, but the thinking behind it is to build in a bit of a safety net in case investments do not grow steadily at the 9% p.a. forecasted. This is a very sensible precaution, because there can be no guarantees.

Source: Clerical Medical

The table shows just one scenario but in practice it is capable of almost infinite adjustment so if, for example, you were confident of getting some income from another source one particular year, you would not need to encash any pensions policies that year.

And what of the drawbacks of such a scheme? The biggest is the obvious one that, to work properly, it requires continuing growth in the pension plans that remain invested. If the growth faltered, all these neat assumptions would be thrown into disarray. Two further points should be borne in mind: because the scheme depends on the 25% cash entitlement each year to provide part of the income, you can never get your hands on one big cash sum at retirement – so you may have to give up your dreams of the round-the-world cruise. And the scheme is only really suitable for those who have substantial pension funds – an absolute minimum of £100,000. Finally, remember that the clock stops at age 75; at this point, Revenue regulations require that the whole of the remaining fund is turned into an annuity.

On the plus side, staggered vesting allows people to draw a pension income from an early age without giving up all potential for investment growth. It avoids the 'investment timing' problem of having to cash in the lot on one particular day. And it has advantages, too, in the event of death before the age of 75, because the balance of the fund (the portion which has not yet been turned into annuities) can be returned to the estate. With annuities, remember, while income is guaranteed for life, once the annuitant dies, no capital is repayable.

4 Income withdrawal or drawdown schemes

There is now one further choice for people to contemplate: an income withdrawal scheme. In essence, this scheme simply allows people to draw an income directly from a special, managed pension fund, in amounts more or less to suit themselves, and to continue doing so until they reach 75 when, once again, the balance must be turned into an annuity. It is possible to take the tax-free cash entitlement of 25% of the total fund; this must be taken at the outset, on retirement, if required.

There are rules on both the maximum and minimum income that can be withdrawn in this way: the maximum is the amount of income that would be produced by a conventional, fixed interest pension annuity for the individual concerned (based on his or her age); the minimum is 35% of the maximum.

This scheme has very similar advantages to the staggered vesting concept in that it allows you to retain the potential for investment growth in your pension fund, which is so vital if you are planning to retire really early. And it also offers some protection in the event of death before age 75. In this case, the balance of the fund can be returned to the estate, although there is a 35% tax charge. Alternatively, if there is a surviving widow or widower, the income withdrawal can continue until the survivor reaches the age of 75 (or the planholder would have been 75, if this is earlier), or it can be turned into an annuity straight away.

The possible disadvantages with the scheme are similar to those of staggered vesting: potential for investment growth inevitably brings with it investment risk. It would probably be unwise to opt for the highest level of income available initially, because this means taking greater risks with the remaining fund. There are in fact automatic checks built in so that, if the fund falls below a certain level at any age, the remaining fund must then be automatically turned into a conventional annuity, even if it happens before you reach 75. Finally, the scheme requires substantial funds (at least £100,000) to be worthwhile unless you also have a decent company pension from a previous job, in which case you might use income withdrawal for a smaller personal pension fund.

The Pensions Choice: Summary

Anyone coming up to retirement has clearly got some hard thinking to do. Of course, you can simply take what is offered by your own pension company when you retire. A quotation for a conventional pension annuity will be provided based on your age (and, if appropriate, that of your spouse), with and without the option of taking the tax-free cash, as well as information on escalating annuities, and possibly index-linked annuities.

But even if you decide that a conventional annuity is what you want, you should still shop around to see if some other pension provider offers a better deal. The answer is almost certain to be 'yes' – and it could mean an improvement of 5 or 10% in your income, every year for life. It is worth consulting a specialist financial adviser at this point because rates change constantly, and it is a full-time job keeping tabs on them all.

If you are retiring young, or have a much younger partner, you should seriously think about options 2, 3 or 4 outlined above. Which is right for you could well depend on other factors, such as the rest of your investments; competent advice is essential.

Finally, as a general rule, whatever type of pension you choose, try to obey the cardinal rule of not being 'too greedy' at the start, by opting for the highest possible income available – in other words, a conventional annuity with level payments. Such a move will condemn you to a steadily decreasing standard of living as inflation takes its toll.

Should you take the tax-free lump sum?

As noted above, personal pensions allow their holders to take 25% of the accumulated fund as a tax-free cash sum on retirement, while the rules on RAPs allow a cash sum of between 25 and 35%, depending on your age at retirement. With these, as with company money purchase-type schemes, the effect of taking the cash is a straightforward one: take 25% in cash, and your remaining pension will be 25% lower than it would otherwise have been.

If you need as high an income as possible, there is a good argument for not taking the cash and retaining the increased pension, but as Table 11 shows, you may be better off using the available cash to buy an ordinary life annuity instead. Life annuities are taxed more lightly than pension annuities, although their underlying rates tend to be slightly worse. Overall, though, basic-rate taxpayers should 'win' by taking the life annuity route.

Table 11: Taking a lump sum

Man aged 65 with £40,000 pension fund	Full pension	Reduced pension + life annuity
Lump sum	Nil	£10,000
Balance	£40,000	£30,000
Buys pension annuity (net of 24% tax)	£3,454 p.a.	£2,583 p.a.
Plus life annuity (net of 20% tax)	Nil	£1,002 p.a.
Total net income	**£3,454 p.a.**	**£3,585 p.a.**

These figures reflect tax rates for the 1996–97 tax year.

Source: Equitable Life

The figures given in Table 11 will depend on age, whether you are married or not and the frequency of payments desired. The life annuity figures will not always work out so advantageously; make sure that you choose a competitive provider for the life annuity because rates do vary markedly, and you could end up the loser. With any type of annuity investors lose access to their capital sum for ever; if you wish to retain this, you might consider some other high income-producing investments, such as Corporate Bond Peps (see Chapter 9, page 98).

Pension problems

Complaints about personal pensions may be dealt with by one of two regulatory bodies. The Personal Investment Authority Ombudsman deals with complaints regarding the selling of a personal pension or (usually) its administration; the Pensions Ombudsman will investigate other matters. For addresses of both organizations, see Appendix I, page 161.

6 ‖ *Insurance after Retirement*

Life Insurance

Life insurance is vital to a young man with a growing family and a large mortgage. The family may be entirely dependent on the income he earns and his premature death could render his widow and children not just penniless but homeless. But people at or approaching retirement are generally past that stage of life, and it is time to reassess what, if any, life cover they might need.

If you have been a member of a company pension scheme you have probably been rather well insured in your later years. Most schemes pay a lump sum on 'death in service' of up to four times annual salary, in addition to a widow(er)'s pension. However, this lump sum cover ceases the day you retire.

So should you replace any of this, and if so, what type of policy should you choose? Life insurance can still be important if:

- you still have large debts such as an outstanding mortgage or a car loan.
- you have continuing financial responsibilities such as university education for children or grandchildren.
- your only significant asset (other than the pension) is your house, which you would like to leave to a son or daughter eventually, but fear they might not be able to pay the possible inheritance tax bill.

Whether it is needed in other cases depends on your own circumstances. If nearly all your retirement income comes from a pension, remember that this is usually cut sharply after the first death. Typically, pensions decline by a third at this point – this is normal practice with company final salary-type schemes. With money purchase schemes and personal pensions, the choice is yours: it is possible, as we have seen in earlier chapters, to opt for pensions that continue at 50%, 67% or 100% of the joint pension. However, few choose the 100% option because this reduces the size of the income considerably.

Many people feel that they would probably want to move home to somewhere smaller and cheaper if their partner were to die before them. In this case, the lower pension income may be no great problem: they will have lower outgoings, as well as a possible profit from 'trading down'. However, few would want to be forced to move immediately, and in any case, it may take time to complete a sale. In view of all this, it is a good idea to have some money in reserve to meet these expenses. If you do not have this in terms of ready cash, the answer may lie in some form of life insurance.

There may also come a time when you are no longer able to care for yourself and have to move into some form of residential home. One way of providing for this eventuality is to take out a long-term care insurance policy (see page 72) but premiums are very expensive and couples may feel that they would be prepared to look after their ailing partner rather than let this happen, in which case the premiums would be wasted. But who would look after the survivor in such a case? Again, a straightforward life assurance policy that pays out a lump sum on the first death might be the best solution.

Whatever type of life insurance policy is chosen, premiums will be relatively expensive compared with those for younger ages. You may be tempted to go for the lowest premiums available for any given sum assured, but be warned: some policies on the market can turn out to be false economies.

Life insurance: the choices

Let us assume you would like a lump sum of £25,000 paid out after the first death. You can opt for a whole of life policy, which guarantees to pay out on the first death whenever that might be, or a term assurance policy, which will pay out only if death occurs within a predetermined term. At first sight, the latter policy may not seem suitable, because there is always the chance you will both survive – in which case you get nothing for your premiums. However, it is possible, at age 60, for example, to take out a term assurance policy of 30 or even 40 years, which will see most of us out.

Table 12 gives some of the best rates currently available on different types of policy. Note that there are two columns of figures given for whole of life policies. The first, cheaper figures relate to policies written on a 'maximum cover basis' and it is these which may prove to be a false economy. With many of these policies the sum assured is only guaranteed at this level if death occurs within 10 years of the policy's inception. Thereafter, both the premium rates and level of cover is reviewed. If you want the premiums to stay the same, this could mean a big reduction in the sum assured. Alternatively, if you want to keep the sum assured at the same level, you may have to accept a significant increase in the premiums charged. This is probably the last thing you would want at the age of 70, particularly if your pension is not fully index-linked, as your real disposable income (after inflation) will have declined in the intervening period. It would be far more sensible to opt for the higher initial premiums charged by either the term assurance or the whole of life policy written on a 'standard cover' basis.

How to choose between the two? In one sense, term assurance is the least risky option, assuming of course that you do not, in fact, live beyond the term chosen. This is because the sum assured is guaranteed, no matter what investment conditions are like. Under the whole of life option, there is an underlying assumption that investment growth within the life fund will average 7.5% a year. If it fails to match this level over the long term, premiums will rise to maintain the same level of cover, although nothing like they would under the maximum cover basis. In any case, over the long term a growth rate of 7.5% is a fairly reasonable assumption.

Table 12: Cost of life assurance

Monthly premiums for £25,000 sum assured

Type of policy	Man aged 60	Woman aged 60	Couple aged 60*
Term: 25 years	£46	£26	£69
Term: 30 years	£51	£29	£76
Term: 40 years	£55	£34	£86
Whole of life:			
Maximum cover	£47	£30	£72
Standard cover	£75	£53	£100

Sum assured payable on first death.

Source: London & Country and Royal Insurance

Shopping around

It is definitely worth shopping around for the most competitive quotes for life assurance. For example, some companies charge in excess of £100 per month for the 25-year term assurance policy for a couple aged 60, compared to the £69 shown here. Similar discrepancies may be found at other ages or terms. If you do not use an insurance broker or other professional adviser to carry out the exercise – which would be a wise idea – do make sure you read the small print. Life companies often use their own brand names for particular types of policy, and it may need a close perusal to work out exactly what type of policy is being offered.

Terminal illness option

Some life companies will now pay out the sum assured either on death or on the diagnosis of a terminal illness. This practice is becoming more common, though it is by no means universal.

Medical examinations

If you are over 60 you should be prepared to undergo a medical examination before being accepted by the life company. Poor results may mean premiums are 'loaded'. An alternative is to opt for a special 'no medical' policy, although premiums will generally speaking be much higher for any given term and sum assured. Unless you are in really poor health, it will always pay to choose a plan where a medical may be required. The purpose of the medical is not necessarily to establish that you are super-fit, merely that you are in normal health for your age. As medical knowledge increases, the definition of 'normal' has in some respects been widened and people who have experienced health problems in the past – breast cancer, for example – can sometimes be accepted at normal rates, or perhaps given only a small loading.

Only if you have significant health problems is it worth going for the 'no medical' option, and even then, it may be worth making two simultaneous applications, one for a non-medical policy and one for a normal policy. Even though the latter may result in premium loadings, the end figure could still be below the premium asked on the former.

Joint life policies
The figures for the joint life policies shown in Table 12 are for a 'joint life first death' policy, which means that the sum assured is paid out after the first of a couple dies. It is also possible to have a 'joint life last survivor' policy, which pays out only on the later death. If you want to provide funds for your partner, the 'first death' option is the one required. However, 'last survivor' policies can provide your ultimate heirs with a cash sum, perhaps to help pay an inheritance tax bill (see page 152).

Life policies and tax
The sum assured payable on death does not in itself attract any form of tax. However, if the money is paid into your estate it might increase a potential inheritance tax charge, so you should ensure the policy is written under a form of trust, which means that the proceeds will be paid out directly to the nominated beneficiaries. Although inheritance tax never gets charged on assets being left by a husband to a wife (or vice versa), there is a further benefit in that

sums assured under a policy written in trust can be paid out directly without waiting for grant of probate.

Endowment policies

There is little point – for most people – in starting an endowment policy after retirement – endowments are, after all, basically savings plans, and the financial emphasis post-retirement switches from saving to spending. However, you may well still have an endowment policy that is not due to mature until some years after retirement. You may be tempted to cash it in and save yourself the monthly outgoings, but this is likely to be bad value for money.

Ideally, you should continue making payments until the policy matures. If your budget does not stretch to this, consider the following options:

- **Making the policy paid-up.** This means that no further premiums are payable, and the policy will mature at its original date (albeit for a reduced sum).
- **Selling the policy on the second-hand endowment market** (suitable for with-profits policies only, not unit-linked policies). You are likely to get a better price for the policy than would be available by surrendering it to the life company. The Association of Policy Marketmakers (see Appendix I, page 164) provides a list of firms which deal in this market. The firms concerned will always establish what the surrender value would be, so you do not run the risk of losing out.

Long-term Care Insurance

Long-term care insurance is the name given to a variety of insurance policies which will pay out if you have to go into a residential or nursing home because you are no longer able to look after yourself. The costs of such homes can be enormous: typically, around £250 a week for a residential home and £350 a week for a nursing home, although in many areas the cost may be much higher.

The State, in this area as in others, provides little in the way of help to those with even modest means. Local authorities do not all follow the same rules in this respect, but basically anyone with assets of £16,000 or more does not qualify for financial help. Some authorities count a house as an asset, others do not. Even when there is a partner still living at home – which obviously makes it impossible to sell the place to meet fees – the authority may place a charge on it, recouping the costs when the property is finally sold.

Clearly, even substantial savings accumulated over a lifetime could be eaten up by fees of £300 a week in a very short time. So is insurance the answer? The insurance industry itself is divided over this. Some companies feel that long-term care insurance (LTC) is going to become a vital part of everyone's armoury against the problems of life. Others have decided that it is simply impossible to produce a scheme which provides value for money. The reason for this division of opinion can be found in the statistics: something like one in four people end up needing some form of residential care. One in four is high enough to make premiums fairly expensive – but not so high as to convince many people that it is worth taking out.

Perhaps the only answer is to be brutally clear-sighted about the matter: do you come from a family whose members live vigorously active lives until 90 and then drop dead? Or do they go into a lengthy decline first? The problem with this approach, of course, is that doctors are getting so much better at patching us up to last another few years that we cannot rely on the fact that our grandparents died smartly at the age of 80. The choice has to be an individual one: there is no right or wrong answer, but do be prepared at least to consider LTC or some alternative arrangements.

How long-term care insurance works

There are two types of policy. One requires monthly premiums, which vary according to your age at the time the policy is taken out. The policy pays out if and only if a valid claim is made. Claims are generally payable when a policyholder becomes unable to carry out three or four (depending on the particular policy) of the following six 'activities of daily living':

- General mobility (the ability to get out of a bed into a chair)
- Dressing
- Eating
- Bathing
- Using the lavatory
- Walking.

Policies will also usually pay out if 'cognitive ability' is impaired to the extent that it is unsafe for an individual to continue living at home. This category could include, for example, sufferers from Alzheimer's Disease.

Premium costs

Table 13 gives sample rates on regular premium policies which will pay out fees of up to £1,000 a month.

Table 13: The cost of long-term care insurance: monthly premiums

Age when policy bought	Man	Woman
60	£52.87	£62.06
65	£71.26	£80.46
70	£93.10	£101.25
75	£111.49	£159.77

Source: PPP Lifetime

One of the problems with these policies is that premiums are expensive, particularly if you wait until you are 70, for example, before taking one out, yet the likelihood is that they will be 'wasted' because most people do not end up needing such care. Even if they do, this type of insurance is not necessarily the best way of paying for it. Suppose, for example, that a woman currently aged 60 does in fact have to go into a residential home at age 85 and dies a year later. Putting £60 a month into some sort of savings scheme during those 25 years would produce a lump sum of £52,000-odd, assuming an average annual growth rate of 7.5%. Of course, residential home fees are likely to have risen with inflation during the 25 years but even so, the annual cost of such care (assuming average inflation at 5% in the intervening period) would only amount to some £44,000. And if she does not in fact need such care, she will be able to leave the £52,000 intact to her heirs.

A halfway house is to opt for a policy which requires a big one-off payment up-front. The cash is then invested by the life company, which deducts from it sufficient premiums to pay for the regular monthly premiums. If the insurance is required, claims will be paid out; if not, there will be a cash-value to the plan on death.

Future developments

The Government recognizes that paying for long-term care is a serious problem. It has announced plans for two developments: firstly, to make company pension plans more flexible, so that people can forego some of their pension in the early years of retirement, to allow them to pay for care in later life, and secondly, to devise some form of partnership scheme, whereby individuals undertake to pay for perhaps the first three years of care, with the Government stepping in afterwards to pick up the bill for the rest. This could cut the cost of LTC premiums by perhaps 20%. Both these developments are currently only in the early planning stages and it may be several years before anything concrete is decided upon.

Private Medical Insurance (PMI)

Many people may have enjoyed private medical cover as a 'perk' from their employer, and be reluctant to go back to the National Health Service after retirement. The good news is that people over the age of 60 qualify for income tax relief on the premiums, and the relief is available for a married couple even if only one of the partners is currently aged over 60, It is, however, restricted to a rate of only 20%, which is automatically deducted from the premiums.

PMI can still be expensive, and careful perusal of the fine print is absolutely essential. There are many different schemes available, with premiums ranging from around £10 a month to more than £100. Here, as in most other things in life, you get what you pay for. Some 'budget' schemes, for example, will only pay for private treatment if the NHS has a waiting list in excess of six weeks. Further restrictions on the type of hospital allowed and the extent of cover help to cut the cost on budget plans. Even with so-called 'comprehensive' cover, there is often a restriction on the total that may be paid out in respect of any one claim.

Table 14 gives some sample premium rates for an 'Over-60' scheme on a comprehensive basis. Rates rise with age, and are also usually reviewed once or twice a year to keep them in line with medical inflation – which has shown a tendency to outpace general price inflation in the last few years. The principal determinant of premium rates is the band of hospital at which you elect to be treated. If you are prepared to pay a proportion of the costs yourself (the 'excess'), premiums can be cut, as the table shows.

Table 14: The cost of private medical insurance

Monthly premiums, net of tax relief, for a couple

Hospital band	Aged 65		Aged 75	
	No excess	£150 excess	No excess	£250 excess
A	£305.11	£250.19	£497.94	£398.35
B	£174.00	£133.98	£278.87	£203.57
C	£136.73	£105.27	£195.77	£142.91

Source: Bupa

Finally, you should note that schemes are unlikely to provide cover for the treatment of existing conditions, although some may do so after a period of years on cover during which you have not made such a claim.

7 | *Investing in Retirement: Where to Find Advice*

Retirement is the time when you stop being a money-making machine in your own right and must look to your pensions and savings to crank out that income for you. With the lump sum available from many pension plans, and perhaps the maturity proceeds of various endowment policies, many people will be faced with what seems like an enormous amount of cash, which must be invested in order to produce the income required.

Of course, you can just put the cash on deposit at a building society, but this is most unlikely to be the best answer. However, not everyone has sufficient knowledge of other areas of investment to feel happy about making their own decisions. Even those who are experts in the field may prefer to let someone else take the strain; I know at least one investment director of a big city firm who believes it is better to let someone else manage his money for him as he has neither the time nor the inclination to do it himself.

By far the most common question asked by readers of *The Sunday Times* is: 'Where can I find a good financial adviser I can trust?' Unless you are an expert yourself, taking advice inescapably means taking things on trust, but recent financial scandals – particularly the mis-selling of personal pensions – have undoubtedly made people suspicious of financial salesmen; after all, they are, in most cases, rewarded for their efforts by receiving commission on products sold, which as a system seems hardly inducive to the provision of completely unbiased advice.

Types of Adviser

Under the Financial Services Act 1986 financial advisers or salesmen are divided into two categories. The first are independent financial advisers, who must look at the whole range of products or services available in the marketplace in order to establish the most appropriate products for a client's needs. The second are employees or 'appointed representatives' of particular companies – generally life assurance companies – who are only allowed to sell or advise on the products of their own company. They cannot even comment on the suitability of anyone else's product.

The Act brought into being a number of 'self-regulatory organizations' or 'financial watchdogs', whose function is to oversee and regulate the activities of their members. Both types of adviser belong, either directly or through their company, to the Personal Investment Authority (PIA). Both must obey a great number of rules and regulations; they are duty-bound to provide advice that is appropriate to their clients' needs, bearing in mind their personal circumstances, financial aims and attitude to risk.

Of the two types, independent advisers should – all other things being equal – be a better choice, simply because they have a wider range of investments to choose from. Some organizations, such as the high street banks, run both types of business. However, unless you specifically request independent advice, you are likely to be directed towards the bank's 'tied' service, where employees may only advise on the bank's own unit trust and life company products.

A third category of financial adviser is the private client stockbroker. Stockbrokers are members of another regulatory organization, the Securities and Futures Authority, which has similar rules for its members, binding them to a duty of care towards their clients. Stockbrokers who cater for private clients can be loosely divided into three categories: those who provide an 'execution-only' service – in other words, merely carry out buying and selling orders without providing any advice; those who are prepared to look after 'small' clients – those with upwards of £20,000 or £30,000 – and who would, in the main, use pooled investments such as unit trusts and investment trusts for the purpose; and those at the top end who prefer their clients to have a minimum of perhaps £250,000 or even £1m to invest (merchant banks are also contenders for such clients' business).

Stockbrokers can be further divided between those offering 'discretionary management' and those providing non-discretionary services. The former describes the situation where clients hand over complete responsibility to the broker to make decisions on their behalf, without consultation (though they are, of course, obliged to inform their clients of what has been done on their behalf). In the latter case, brokers will provide advice, but will not initiate any action unless specifically requested to do so by the client. Generally speaking, 'discretionary management' is the more practical and less costly option for both parties.

Some financial advisory firms, whether they be stockbrokers or other types of financial adviser, may also belong to IMRO (the Investment Managers Regulatory Organization), if their business is solely concerned with the managing of investments, rather than other aspects of financial planning, such as tax.

Finally, some firms of registered insurance brokers also have a general financial planning arm, as do some firms of accountants and solicitors. Depending on the amount of financial business they do, they may be regulated either by their own professional body (such as the Law Society, the Chartered Institute of Accountants and the Insurance Brokers Registration Council) or have a subsidiary business which is regulated by the PIA. All firms must carry information on their stationery stating which organization they are regulated by.

Paying for advice

All advice costs money, but some of these costs are more hidden than others. Life company employees generally get commission on products sold; 'non-commission paying' companies may pay their employees a salary but still give their employees sales targets to meet. Independent financial advisers usually earn their living by commission, though a growing number will charge fees instead and rebate any commission to their client. Stockbrokers who provide advice can follow either route; some give clients the choice of either fees or commission.

Commission disclosure

Since the beginning of 1995 all life assurance companies have been obliged to disclose the commission payable on their products to everyone who buys them, along with full details of the charges that are being deducted. They will be joined by all unit trust companies in the summer or autumn of 1996. This is undoubtedly a beneficial development, but the figures themselves are not likely to be of any particular use to buyers. Knowing that a particular product pays, say, £100 in commission to the seller does not get the purchaser very far. How much would another similar product pay – more or less? Are you getting a 'bargain' or paying through the nose? Is it fair payment for the time the adviser has spent on your case or not? None of these questions is answered by the figure itself.

Any type of cost may be off-putting to people who, hitherto, have dealt only with building societies for their financial needs, because there appears to be no cost involved in opening a building society account. Of course, if one compares the mortgage rate charged to borrowers with the interest rate paid to savers, it becomes evident that the true cost lies in this gap. Commission disclosure is, nevertheless, proving good for customers because it is forcing companies to be more competitive and to cut charges. There are still many areas where the state of things is less than satisfactory, but matters are improving.

Commission versus charges

What is of real importance to the buyer of financial products is not the commission payable to a seller, but the overall charges levied on the product. These, too, must be disclosed to buyers, although, again, it may be difficult to judge whether something is 'expensive' or 'cheap. In the chapters that follow, the impact of charges will be made clear in relation to particular products.

How to find an adviser

The organization IFA Promotion runs an information service to direct people towards their nearest independent financial adviser. Enquirers should write to IFAP at Studio House, 5–7 Flowers Hill, Brislington, Bristol BS4 5JJ, or telephone 0117 971 1177 with details of their post code. They will be sent a list of six advisory companies picked on the basis of their proximity to the enquirer's home or office.

Every company on the list submits to IFAP a brief description of its business and any specialization it may have, which will be provided to enquirers – although this description is written by the firm itself, and there is no 'quality control'. Moreover, the list only covers those independent advisers who actually subscribe to IFAP – at the last count, around 75% of the total number in existence.

The IFAP list makes no distinction between advisers who get paid by commission and those who charge fees. However, the specialist magazine *Money Management* runs a National Directory of Fee-based Advisers, which will provide enquirers with a list of six names and addresses, again on the basis of geographical proximity, all of whom charge for their services through fees. Furthermore, you can stipulate that you would like firms specializing in particular areas, such as tax or investment. There are about 850 firms in total listed. While regular checks are made that the firms concerned still belong to their appropriate regulatory organization, no other type of vetting is carried out. The telephone number for the directory is 0117 976 9444 and the address for written enquiries is: National Directory of Fee-based Advisers, Matrix Data Services, Freepost, Gossard House, 7–8 Savile Row, London W1X 1AF.

The Stock Exchange runs a public information line which will send out details of brokers' names and addresses on 0171 797 1448, and finally, the Association of Private Client Investment Managers and Stockbrokers (APCIMS) provides a complete list of its 135-strong membership with details of the services they offer. Write to: APCIMS, 112 Middlesex Street, London E1 7HY.

Choosing an adviser

There is no magic route to finding the perfect adviser. It actually helps if you know a little bit about the issues yourself, largely because that will give you more confidence to ask questions on matters that have not been made clear, and to judge the value of the answers given. Never be afraid to ask such questions; if you have not understood something the first time, that is a failure on the part of the adviser to explain the matter properly.

You must also be prepared for some in-depth grilling on the state of your financial affairs and your aims and attitudes. Not only is this required by law under the Financial Services Act; no sensible adviser expects to give proper advice without knowing your full background. It is only sensible to be realistic in your choice of adviser, and to expect him or her to be realistic with you; if your investment portfolio totals £10,000 it is a waste of your adviser's time (and probably your money) to insist on management by some gold-plated merchant bank.

Other rules on choosing a good adviser boil down to these: distrust advisers who tell you they are always right; or who claim that they can make you rich overnight; and finally, trust your own instincts. If, after a lengthy meeting with an adviser, you feel that you do not really like him or her, then find someone else – it's as simple as that.

If Things Go Wrong

All regulatory organizations have formal procedures in place to deal with complaints arising between an adviser and its clients. The general rule is that both parties must make an effort to resolve the issue first. Only once impasse has been reached – which in effect means when the client has been finally turned down by the organization's chief executive – can the regulatory organization step in. The company is duty-bound to inform clients of how the complaints procedure works and who to contact; see also Appendix I (page 161) for addresses and contact numbers.

Complaints normally have to be raised within six years (or within three years from the time the person concerned first realized that there was matter for complaint). In addition, the regulatory organizations generally impose a rule that complainants must contact them within six months of getting a final 'no' on their complaint from the company concerned.

8 ‖ *Planning Your Post-retirement Portfolio 1: Low Risk Investments*

Investment planning is usually an exercise in achieving the best possible compromise between conflicting aims. All investors would like to put their money in an investment producing a high and rising yield, good growth in capital, with no risk and tax-free. Of course, no investment provides this: some provide high immediate yields, but little or no prospect of growth: others provide potential for growth but with risk attached.

Stocktaking for Inflation

As a first step in planning your portfolio, you need to take an inventory of your assets, income and liabilities. Your liabilities – except for repayment of existing debts – you may assume will on the whole increase in line with inflation. But what of your income? Start with your pension: to what extent, if any, is this going to increase to match inflation? Someone retiring at State pension age, for example, is likely to have a pension income from a number of sources: basic State pension; the State Earnings Related Pension scheme; and a company or personal pension. State pensions are guaranteed to be index-linked. Company pensions may or may not be index-linked: those paid by big companies are likely to rise fully in line with inflation, while pensions paid by the Government to its employees are guaranteed to do so.

However, if you are retiring from a company money purchase scheme, or with a personal pension, you may have opted either for a rising pension or a level one.

Remember that even 'index-linked' pensions rise in line with prices rather than incomes. Since, in the past, earnings have always tended to increase at a faster rate than prices, even those on an RPI-linked pension may feel poorer as the years go by – and if your standard of living is declining relative to that of the working population, there is a sense in which you would indeed be poorer. A recent survey published by the Joseph Rowntree Foundation showed that whereas in the early 1980s only a quarter of pensioners thought the basic State pension 'really low', this proportion had risen to 40% by the early 1990s.

It is impossible, however, to obtain a pension guaranteed to rise in line with earnings, and in any case, the cards are not all stacked against retired people. Many, having paid for their homes and brought up their children, will have cast off so many of the liabilities that burden the middle-aged, that perceptions of relative poverty will scarcely affect them.

So an income that rises 'only' in line with prices may not be such a bad thing after all. But do be clear: an income that does *not* have

Table 15: Real value of £100 today, after inflation at the following rates

Years	3%	4%	5%
1	£97.08	£96.15	£95.24
5	£86.26	£82.29	£78.35
10	£74.41	£67.56	£61.35
15	£64.19	£55.53	£48.10
20	£55.36	£45.64	£37.69
25	£47.76	£37.51	£29.53

Table 16: Average rates of inflation

AVERAGE RECENT RATES			AVERAGE RATES IN THE PAST		
Term	Dates		Term	Dates	
5 years	1990–94	4.95%	5 years	1975–79	15.68%
10 years	1985–94	4.99%	5 years	1980–84	10.58%
20 years	1975–94	8.97%	5 years	1985–89	5.03%
			10 years	1975–84	13.10%

such a guarantee does indeed mean that, year by year, your standard of living will fall. At today's rates of inflation the process is relatively slow – but the effects build up alarmingly over time. Table 15 shows the effect that even today's 'low' rates of inflation have on purchasing power over the years, while Table 16 shows the average level of inflation over various periods.

Planning Your Portfolio: the Layered Approach

It is a basic maxim of financial planning that money should be spread among different types of investment, with different degrees of risk. There are three basic building blocks, or asset classes: 'cash' (by which is meant, not the folding stuff itself, but bank deposit accounts and similar products), fixed interest securities, and equities (company shares). Table 17 is a thumbnail sketch, highlighting the main differences between the three.

Table 17: Asset classes

Cash	*Fixed interest*	*Equities*
Building society and bank accounts, Tessas, National Savings Income Bonds, etc.	Gilts, corporate bonds, Pibs, etc.	Income unit trusts, Peps, investment trust income shares, with-profit bonds, etc.
Capital Security:		
High	Medium	Low
Income Yield (gross):		
High	High	Low
6–7.5%	7–9%	3–5%
Growth potential – income:		
None (may rise or fall)	None	High
Growth potential – capital:		
None	Low	High

Only investments within the 'cash' class offer 100% capital security and a reasonable starting yield; but only equities offer the potential for a growing income, together with the potential for capital growth. On the other hand, equities offer the lowest immediate income, and for all their 'potential', there is, of course, risk: the capital and the income may fall in value.

Nevertheless, in the end, one can only point to history to show that, over the long term, equities will handsomely outpace any competing investment. Figures 2 and 3 tell exactly the same story, except that the first shows what has happened in money terms, while the second – to which one should pay closer attention – illustrates the results in 'real' terms, after adjustment for inflation.

You may conclude from this that everyone should have as much as possible in equity-related investments, but what is possible depends largely on individuals' own particular circumstances: those whose pension income is relatively low may be obliged to put more of their remaining assets into cash or fixed interest securities, because these provide a higher immediate income. 'Psychological possibility' will be another factor: if putting your capital at risk would give you sleepless nights, then there is little sense in doing so, however good an investment it is. If you think you are in this category, do nevertheless read the rest of this book first as it may serve to change your mind.

Finally, it makes sense to have at least some of your assets in a capital secure environment to ensure a proper spread of risk, and also as a home for the money you will or may need to spend later – on holidays, for example, or unexpected emergencies.

Many investments which offer complete capital security also provide a variable rate of interest. The general rule is that the longer the term of notice you are prepared to give, and the larger the sum invested, the higher the going rate of interest. Thus, for example, at the time of writing, the Halifax is offering 4.35% gross on its instant access, Liquid Gold account, but 5.6% on its 60-day notice, Bonus Gold account – both rates for minimum sums of £10,000. For sums of £100,000-plus, the Bonus Gold rate rises to 6.35%.

Some other investments, such as National Savings Certificates,

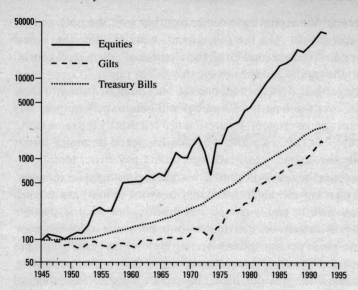

Figure 2: Equity investment, gross income reinvested *Source:* BZW

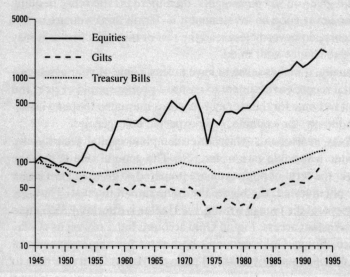

Figure 3: Equity Investment, gross income reinvested in real terms
Source: BZW

offer risk-free capital and a fixed rate of interest. Since few people can successfully guess in which direction interest rates might move over time, it makes sense to spread your risk within the category of secure investments, with some at a variable rate, and some fixed rate.

Secure Capital: Variable Interest

Bank and building society accounts
It pays to check periodically that you are getting the most competitive rates on your bank or building society accounts. *The Sunday Times* carries a table each week of the highest rates available for different notice periods and minimum investments, so look at least once a year and see whether your accounts are still paying reasonable rates. Societies can and do adjust their rates for marketing reasons as well as when there is a general change in interest rates; it has been estimated that, in total, savers 'lose' up to £800m a year by keeping their money in uncompetitive building society accounts, or current accounts that do not pay any interest (not surprisingly, building societies do not give out any figures in this respect).

The newspapers can only provide a summary of the best rates, but a monthly publication entitled *Moneyfacts* lists interest rates on all available accounts from banks and building societies. For the address see Appendix I (page 163).

While everyone should have their 'emergency kitty' in an account where they can obtain cash instantly without giving notice, it will clearly pay to have as much of the 'secure' portion of your portfolio as possible in a more remunerative home, where longer periods of notice are required, or where the investment has a fixed term.

Tax Exempt Special Savings Accounts (Tessas)
Tessas are suitable for just about everyone, the reason being simply that they are tax-free and therefore provide higher returns

to any taxpayer than ordinary taxed investments. There are now two types of Tessa: the first is for those who have not had one before, while the second is designed for those who are coming to the end of Tessa mark one. Different rules apply to each.

Tessa (1): A maximum of £9,000 may be invested over a period of five years. In the first year, up to £3,000 may be invested; in subsequent years, a maximum of £1,800 per year (if you have invested these maximum sums in years one to four, you will be limited to a total of £600 in the final year). As long as no capital is withdrawn during the five-year term, the interest is free of tax. However, holders can withdraw interest during the term, which is paid net of a notional basic rate tax charge – with the balance of interest rolling up and being paid out with the capital on completion of the term.

Tessa (2): Once the first Tessa has matured, investors have six months in which to decide whether or not to save for a further five years. The full capital sum invested in the first Tessa, up to £9,000, may be invested in a lump sum in a new edition Tessa, which can be with either the original provider, or a different one. Rolled-up interest cannot be reinvested, and no additional sums may be added. As with the first Tessa, interest net of a notional basic-rate tax charge may be withdrawn each year, but capital must remain invested for the full five years in order to reap the tax concession.

Most Tessa providers pay a variable rate of interest but a few offer fixed rates – either for one year or for the full five-year term.

National Savings Income Bonds
Interest on these is variable; at the time of writing, it is 6.5% for investments up to £25,000 and 6.75% for larger investments (to the maximum £250,000). Income is paid out monthly, gross, but is taxable. Three months' notice is required for withdrawals.

Secure Capital: Fixed Interest

National Savings Certificates: fixed rate and index-linked
These are five-year investments where returns are free of tax. No income is paid during the term; it is rolled up to produce a bigger capital sum on maturity.

Rates available on the fixed interest certificates vary from time to time – at the time of writing the current issue is the 42nd, paying a fixed annual rate of 5.85% for five years. While you can withdraw capital earlier, the price is a significant reduction in interest paid – withdrawals during the first year mean no interest at all is payable.

The index-linked certificates pay a fixed supplement in addition to inflation during their five-year term; the current (8th) issue offers 3% plus inflation. Again, there are penalties for earlier encashment.

Because interest is tax-free, both types of certificate offer the best value to higher-rate taxpayers: someone liable to 40% tax would have to obtain in excess of 9.75% gross to better their net return from the 42nd issue – and this is simply not available elsewhere with such a cast-iron guarantee. Non-taxpayers, by contrast, can usually obtain better rates elsewhere; the rates are generally pitched to make the terms reasonably competitive for basic-rate taxpayers, who will need to shop around carefully before deciding whether these are the best investments for them at any one time.

If fixed interest certificates are not cashed in at the end of their five-year term, they continue to attract tax-free interest, but on a variable basis known as the General Extension Rate. This is always pitched below the rate on the current issue – it stands today at 3.51% – so it does not pay to leave your money there once the fixed term has expired.

National Savings Pensioners' Guaranteed Income Bond
This pays monthly interest at a fixed rate for a five year term; the interest is paid gross but is taxable. The current 2nd series

pays 7.5% per year. It is only available to people over the age of 60.

Guaranteed Income Bonds

These bonds are issued by life companies and pay a fixed rate for their term, which may be anything from one to five years. Income is paid out, usually once a year, and net of basic-rate tax which cannot be reclaimed by non-taxpayers; higher-rate taxpayers must pay extra. Rates for basic-rate taxpayers are usually very competitive. It is a good idea to check what happens if the bondholder dies during the year, between income payments: some bonds pay out interest pro-rata; others pay nothing at all. For those who do not need income paid out, there is often a growth option, allowing interest to be accumulated until the end of the term.

Details of current offers can generally be found in the round-up of top savings rates published each week by newspapers such as *The Sunday Times*.

Gilts held to maturity

Government securities, known as 'gilts', pay a fixed rate of interest during their life. Gilts are negotiable securities, which means you do not have to buy them at the time they were issued, but can purchase them from another holder via the Stock Exchange. Unless the gilts are bought on issue, purchasers must pay the going rate at any one time, which is influenced by the general level of interest rates.

For example, at the time of writing, it actually cost £120.90 to buy £100 nominal of stock of Treasury 11.75% 2003–7, because interest rates have moved down since the stock was first issued. At this price the 'running yield' on the stock – the amount of income you get each year before it matures – works out at 9.77% a year. However, because the stock will only be redeemed at £100, there is a guaranteed capital loss awaiting you at that time. Building this into the calculation produces the 'redemption yield', which in this case works out at 8%.

Firms of stockbrokers routinely crunch these numbers – on a daily basis, as prices move – and are best placed to advise those wishing to invest in gilts. They may also be bought, more cheaply, via the National Savings Stock Register. A booklet on the Register is available at post offices. The drawback to buying through the Register is that you do not know the price you have paid until the stock has actually been purchased for you.

Different types of gilts: Gilts are differentiated both by the length of term they have to run until redemption, and also by their nominal interest rate (the 'coupon'). Short-dated gilts have up to five years to run; medium-dated ones, between five and 15 years, and long-dated gilts have terms in excess of 15 years. There are also a few 'undated' gilts, which in practice will probably last for ever.

The majority of gilts are 'high coupon', which means that, at issue, the Government offered to pay what was then the going rate of interest, and asked investors to pay £100 of money for each £100 'nominal' of stock. But there are some issues of 'low coupon' gilts available. Here, the interest rate seems very low – between 2 and 3% – but the difference is that the price paid for £100 nominal stock is much lower. If investors pay £30 for stock they know is going to be redeemed in 10 years' time, say, at £100, then they will be prepared to accept a much lower interest rate in the meantime in return for the eventual capital gain. Low coupon gilts tend to be suitable for higher-rate taxpayers, because the eventual gain will be tax-free, whereas income would be taxed at a high rate.

Index-linked gilts are a different animal altogether, and they are unique in the investment world, being the only genuinely risk-free investment (along with their National Savings' equivalent, the index-linked certificates). Income returns are guaranteed to retain their real value after inflation, as is the capital value, so long as investors keep the gilts until redemption. (If they sell in the meantime then, like any other tradeable security, the price may vary depending on the current market.) The drawback with index-linked gilts is that the initial level of income available is very low, perhaps around 2% gross.

Other Capital Secure Investments

Guaranteed equity bonds

This is the general name given to a variety of investment products, all of which use financial futures or options of some type to provide a combination of guaranteed capital together with some exposure to possible future growth in the stock market. The underlying structure of these bonds can be very complex and – for the financial layman – extremely difficult to understand. They are, in effect, a halfway house for investors who would like to benefit from stock market growth but are unwilling to risk the security of their capital; they have proved extremely popular with investors.

Nevertheless, there is a price to be paid for the guarantee. A typical product, currently available, is a five-year bond which promises investors 100% of any rise in the FT-SE 100 Index from inception to end of the term. If the index falls over this period, investors are guaranteed their money back in full.

This might sound wonderful, but there are two disadvantages: firstly, the investment earns no interest or income during the term and secondly, if the stock market were to rise between the start and end date, but fall back by the end to where it started, investors would not be able to profit by selling out early.

There are a number of different variations on this theme – some will guarantee a return of, say, 140% of investors' original capital at the end of the five years, but offer only half the growth in the index during the term. Others offer a lock-in facility, so that if the market rises strongly mid-term, investors can 'lock in' to the gain already achieved. The tax structure of the bonds also differs: some are life assurance bonds, others based offshore; this has varying implications for basic- and higher-rate taxpayers.

While the concept behind all these products is attractive, anyone who is prepared for some medium-term risk to capital is likely to do better by opting for a straightforward investment in the stock market, particularly if they can do so tax-free by means of a Personal Equity Plan (see page 107). Suppose, for example, the market does, in the event, rise by 25% over the following five years. Investing in the guaranteed bond of the first type described above would yield basic-rate taxpayers a profit of exactly 25%; a Pep-holder could expect an additional profit of perhaps 15 to 20%, representing the reinvested dividends.

These bonds are generally limited issues, and terms can change overnight. It is wise to get independent professional advice before choosing which particular product to buy.

Credit Risk

To describe any investment as 'risk-free' is perhaps erroneous, in that there is always the possibility (however remote) that the organization which holds your money will go bust. Investors should at least be aware of the limits of the various compensation schemes in existence.

- **National Savings products:** guaranteed by the Government. No other guarantee, or compensation scheme, necessary – or possible.
- **Building societies:** the compensation scheme provides 90% of the first £20,000 invested. The limit is per person, per society.
- **Banks:** 90% of the first £20,000 of deposits are protected per person in the event of any bank going bust.
- **Insurance companies:** the Policyholders Protection Act provides for compensation of 100% of the first £30,000 and 90% of the next £20,000 in the event of an insurance company collapse.
- **Other compensation:** the Investors Compensation Scheme established under the Financial Services Act provides protection for investors where a financial company has had a

complaint against it upheld by one of the regulatory bodies or Ombudsmen, and where an award has been made to the investor. If the firm proves unable to pay and goes into liquidation, the ICS kicks in, providing maximum compensation per individual of £48,000, representing 100% of the first £30,000 followed by 90% of the next £20,000.

No scheme compensates people for losses incurred through normal investment risk except, under the ICS, where it can be proved that the individual was wrongfully advised to buy particular products bearing in mind their aims, financial circumstances and attitudes at the time of purchase. The fact that something turns out to be a poor investment is not proof that the advice to invest in it was wrong.

Interest and Tax

From the beginning of the 1996–97 tax year, basic-rate taxpayers will pay tax at a rate of only 20% on the interest arising from most investments, including bank and building society accounts, gilts, and those National Savings products such as Income Bonds and Pensioners Bonds where the interest is gross but taxable.

In most cases, the interest will be paid out net of the 20% tax, and basic-rate taxpayers will have no further liability. Higher-rate taxpayers, however, will have to make up the full difference to their 40% rate. In other words, they must pay an additional 20% tax, compared to the 15% charge made in previous years.

9 ‖ *Planning Your Post-retirement Portfolio 2: Fixed Interest and Other Medium Risk Investments*

The investments which occupy the next step up on the risk ladder are a mixed bunch. They include gilts that are not held to maturity, corporate bond funds and with-profits bonds: there is no absolute guarantee with any of these investments that capital will be returned intact, but they are not as risky as equity investments, and the returns from such investments over the years will be likely to fall somewhere between the 'no risk' and the 'high risk' plans.

Gilts

In the last chapter we saw that gilts can only provide predictable returns if they are held until maturity. Should you sell before that date, the price received will reflect the going rate for interest at that time. If interest rates have risen since you bought, you will make a loss; if they have fallen, you will make a profit. Few private investors buy and sell gilts themselves on a regular basis; however, such holdings may well be part of a managed portfolio run by stockbrokers, who will take profits on gilts that have risen markedly in value since purchase.

Income-seeking investors should remember, however, that gilts will only rise in value if interest rates have fallen – so while you might be able to realize a profit, you would not be able to reinvest elsewhere to provide the same rate of income as you had obtained from the gilt.

Corporate Bonds

What they are

When companies need money, they have three main choices: to raise it by borrowing from the banks, by issuing new share capital, or by issuing 'corporate bonds', which are fixed interest securities, similar in their workings to gilts. Because companies – however big and blue chip – are not such a good credit risk as the Government, they must offer a slightly higher interest rate than the going rate on gilts to entice investors to put up their money. They will, naturally enough, try to get away with paying the very minimum; bonds issued by the biggest companies will pay perhaps 20 to 25 basis points above a similar gilt (0.2% to 0.25%), while smaller and less solid companies may have to pay up to 200 basis points (2%) a year more.

Who they are suitable for

Bonds can be very good investments for income-seeking investors, but what makes them really interesting is that they may now be put into a Personal Equity Plan (Pep), so that investors can receive the income tax-free. Individuals are allowed to invest a maximum of £6,000 a year of new money into a General Pep containing such bonds, but they may also switch monies held in previous years' Peps into the new bond Peps if desired. Anyone seeking to increase the income yield from their portfolio at or around retirement may well be advised to follow this course.

Bond Peps: how to choose

Within three months of the authorization for bond Peps coming into force, at least 40 different funds were launched, making the choice difficult. The first point to check is the yield. Two yield figures will be quoted: an estimated annual yield, which shows the level of income investors can expect on their investment; and an estimated redemption yield, which takes into account the loss (or gain) to their capital if all the bonds in the portfolio were held until their maturity. The two figures are likely to be similar, although at the present time the redemption yield may well be slightly below the annual yield. A big gap between the two means in effect that investors who withdraw all the income will be eating into their capital.

At the time of writing yields on these Peps vary between about 7% and 8.5%. The difference will be largely accounted for by the different companies in which the Pep managers choose to invest; the higher the rate, the more risky the underlying bonds are perceived to be by the stock market, which has priced them accordingly.

Investors should also pay close attention to the charges levied on the Pep. These may include an initial charge, an annual management charge and possibly an 'exit' charge as well. Fierce competition between providers has already cut charges to some extent, but some products are more expensive than others. Active investment management may possibly provide better returns, but you will certainly benefit from lower charges.

Some bond Peps promise that they will only invest in bonds which are top rated by the major credit-rating agencies, such as Standard & Poors; others are prepared to cast their net more widely. Investors should also consider the impact of active management on the income-stream. If you buy a single bond within a 'self select Pep' and hold it until maturity, the level of income will remain fixed throughout the term. But if managers are actively buying and selling bonds, the income level will fluctuate. If you need a guaranteed level of income, it may be worth going for a self select bond Pep, which are run by a number of private client stockbrokers. With such a Pep, investors will not get the spread of risk provided by a fund; their Pep may include no more than two or three companies' bonds (any more, and the costs will outweigh the benefits). Nevertheless, if they stick to big blue chip companies, the risk should be relatively low.

Bond Peps and capital risk

Investors must be prepared to give up complete capital security if they invest in bonds. There are three types of capital risk: firstly (and worst), the company they invest in may go into liquidation, losing them all their capital. Readers may well remember the collapse of Barings Bank, when a number of private bondholders lost their entire capital. Buying a bond fund effectively negates this risk, because funds are likely to hold stock from at least 20 different companies (and probably many more) so that no more than 5% of their capital would be at risk if any one company folded.

Secondly, the value of the bond or the fund will move from day to day as the market responds to changes in the level of supply and demand, or as underlying interest rates move upwards or downwards. Investing in a single bond will guarantee the level of income an investor receives during its life, but will not fix the level of capital during that time.

Thirdly, the higher the immediate income a fund provides, the more likely it is that the underlying bonds will be priced 'over par'. This means that one is buying income at the expense of capital; the difference between the running, or annual yield, and the redemption yield, is an indication of this.

Despite these caveats, bond Peps are a strong contender for a place in the retirement portfolios of many investors.

Building Society Permanent Interest Bearing Shares (Pibs)

What they are
Building societies also need to raise capital from time to time, and the big ones are allowed to do so by issuing Pibs. In most respects Pibs are similar to gilts or company bonds except that they are 'permanent'; in other words, the society need never pay back the capital. Investors who want to get their money out must sell them on the stock market, where the price they receive will depend on general investment conditions at the time.

Who they are suitable for
The attraction of Pibs is the level of income they pay: at the time of writing, for example, a purchase of Bradford & Bingley's 13%

Pibs (at the price then ruling) would yield 10.09% gross, compared to 6.15% gross from that society's 30-day notice account. Pibs cannot be put into a Pep, so tax must be paid on the interest. However, couples planning their retirement portfolio might be able to arrange matters so that the partner who has little income in his or her own right – typically, the wife who has not built up a pension of her own – could hold the Pibs and thus escape with little or no tax to be paid. Pibs income is (from April 1996) paid out net of 20% tax, which may be reclaimed by non-taxpayers; basic-rate taxpayers have nothing further to pay, while higher-rate taxpayers must pay an additional 20% tax.

How to choose
Pibs cannot be purchased directly from a building society; they must be bought through a stockbroker, who should be able to provide advice on the most suitable issues. Some will effectively be ruled out for many private investors because their minimum investment is so high – Halifax Pibs, for example, require a minimum of £50,000 nominal stock to be purchased.

Pibs and capital risk
Pibs are not like ordinary building society investments: capital will fluctuate along with the general level of interest rates, while there is also the remote risk that a society might go bust. Once purchased, however, like any other fixed interest security, the income stream will be guaranteed so long as the investor continues to hold the security. Pibs holders should qualify for any bonuses or share issues if the society concerned is bought out or goes public, which will mean a windfall gain.

Investment Trust Income Shares

What they are
Investment trusts are companies which invest in other companies' shares. Their own share capital may be split into various different

types of share. The simplest split is between income shares, which get all the income from the underlying portfolio, but none of the growth, and growth shares, which get all the growth and none of the income. If the split between the two types of share is equal, income shareholders will benefit from an income level that is twice the going rate; moreover, the income is likely to rise over the years along with the general growth in company dividends.

Who they are suitable for

Income shares are a good choice for people who, at retirement, need not only a high level of income from their savings now, but also some built-in protection against the effects of inflation over the years.

Capital risk

Capital is not secure in investment trust income shares; indeed, in most cases investors are guaranteed a capital loss when the trust comes to the end of its life and shareholders are paid back their money. Some income shares will pay back a fixed amount per income share of perhaps £1 or 50p; others, known as 'annuity income shares' pay back nothing at all – or a nominal amount of 1p. This does not necessarily mean they are bad investments; the amount of income received in the intervening period should compensate investors for their loss of capital. It does mean, however, that great care should be taken in the choice of share because the precise terms – the length of the trust's life, the split between income, capital and other types of share, and the terms on which capital (if any) is repaid to income shareholders – are extremely important.

How to choose

The factors mentioned above make it highly advisable for investors to seek professional advice before buying such stocks. Private client stockbrokers are the best source of such advice.

Other Split Capital Investment Trust Shares

The other most common types of split capital shares are growth (or capital) shares, which generally get none of the income but all the growth from an underlying portfolio. A split trust may also include 'Zero Dividend Preference Shares', which provide a predetermined rate of growth for their holders during the life of the trust, assuming certain investment conditions are met. There are almost countless variations along these themes. Because neither growth shares nor Zeros pay an income, they are unlikely to find their way into retirement portfolios, but they may interest investors who have significant assets and are seeking to maximize tax-efficiency.

With-Profits Bonds

What they are
With-profits bonds are lump sum investments issued by life assurance companies. The with-profits fund is generally invested in a mixture of company shares, commercial property and gilts, making it a very widely spread and relatively low risk home for cash. In addition, with-profits funds are deliberately run to achieve a 'smoothing' effect over the years: some of the profits earned on the fund in the form of reserves are kept back to help push up returns to policyholders when investment conditions are bad. The bonds are in effect a lump sum version of the regular premium with-profits endowment policy, which many people put their savings into during their working lives, perhaps as the means to pay off their mortgage.

Who they are suitable for
With-profits bonds allow investors to take a regular 'income' from their investment of about 7.5% a year. This is net of basic-rate tax, which cannot be reclaimed by non-taxpayers. Higher-rate tax-payers face an additional charge, but it is relatively low, as the tax rules allow bondholders to withdraw 5% a year for a period of 20

years tax-free. This means that higher-rate tax only has to be paid on the remaining 2.5% of the payout.

Capital security

The 'income' payment is not quite what it seems, and should not be compared directly to a deposit account. Bondholders' returns will be made up partly of interest or dividends paid on the underlying investments, and partly from capital growth, so bondholders are in effect drawing out some of their capital profits as income each year. If the fund's investments consistently failed to meet the rate at which withdrawals are made, then investors would be eating into their capital. Companies reserve the right to impose what is called a Market Value Adjustment Factor (MVAF): techno-speak for cutting down the amount of capital it will pay back if you realize the investment.

That said, the bonds should still be viewed as a low to medium risk investment. Companies have rarely imposed this adjustment factor, and the with-profits fund is run conservatively with a view to avoiding such cuts if possible.

How to choose

Investors should take a number of factors into account before choosing which company's bond to buy. Least important is the rate of 'income' offered; companies can, in effect, choose whatever rate they like. A higher rate simply means you are taking a greater risk with your capital. While good investment management can produce higher returns, the difference is unlikely to be very great over time.

Factors to be assessed include the overall strength of the company's reserves and its record of paying out annual bonuses. It would be wise to consult an independent financial adviser before choosing.

Medium Risk Investments: Overall Planning Points

The investments described here all involve some risk to investors' capital. The reward is, generally speaking, a higher income than can be obtained from deposit-type investments. But there is also another advantage to be gained by taking some of your assets out of cash and into fixed interest or other types of security. With variable rate cash deposits investors are prey to movements in interest rates. If they fall, investors' income is immediately cut and there is no compensation. Indeed, building society investors found this out the hard way in the early 1990s when they saw income from their savings more than halved over a period of about four years.

But falling interest rates are generally good news for gilts and bonds, as well as for the equity markets, and at such times investors are generally compensated by a rise in capital values. Those trying to protect the overall worth of their investment portfolio (and its capacity to produce income) in the years ahead should ensure that they spread their risk. It would be just as imprudent for investors to put all their savings into corporate bond Peps, for example, as it would for them to keep everything in a variable rate savings account.

However, this is not the end of the story: we have not yet really tackled one of the most important objectives of investing for retirement: securing an income that will grow over the years to meet or outpace inflation. For that we must turn to equities.

10 ‖ *Planning Your Post-retirement Portfolio 3: Higher Risk Investments for a Growing Income*

All retirement portfolios should contain some investments which are capable of providing a growing income. Interest from banks and building societies will rise or fall over the years according to the general level of interest rates; income from gilts and bonds will stay fixed at the level at which you bought them – which may prove to be comfortably high or disastrously low. To protect your income against the ravages of long-term inflation, then (apart from index-linked gilts) the only answer is to invest in equities – company shares.

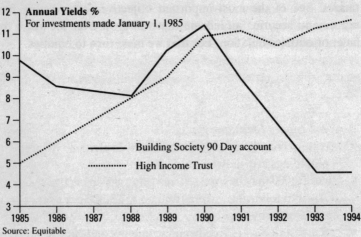

Source: Equitable

Figure 4: Growing income from a unit trust

Figure 4 shows how an income from shares can, over time, beat a building society account by providing that all-important growth.

The chart assumes an investment was made just over 10 years ago in 1985, and tracks the level of income available from that investment compared to the return paid out by a building society. Note that the chart shows only what has happened to income payments, but capital, too, will have risen in value in the case of the shares; capital in the building society, meanwhile, will have stayed fixed.

The younger people are when they retire, the more important it is for their portfolio to contain a significant element of 'growing income' investments. For such people – those retiring at or before the age of 60 – there may even be a case for having two different retirement portfolios, Mark One to see you through the first 10 to 15 years of retirement, and Mark Two to cater for your needs in later life, when a shift from equities towards fixed interest investments may be appropriate. (This topic is dealt with in Chapter 12.)

How to Buy Company Shares

There are a number of ways in which you can invest in company shares. You can buy individual shares through a stockbroker, or opt for one of the pooled investment vehicles such as unit or investment trusts. As long as certain rules are obeyed, any of these investments can be put into Personal Equity Plans, which means that all returns, whether of income or capital growth, will be tax-free.

Personal Equity Plans: the rules
- Investors must be over 18 and resident in Britain. No joint Pep holdings are allowed.
- Up to £6,000 may be invested in a general Pep each tax year (6 April to following 5 April) and up to £3,000 per year in a Single Company Pep.
- Pep investments are free from income tax and capital gains tax; income may be withdrawn gross and tax-free. On the death of the Pep holder, no capital gains tax is payable on disposals but the proceeds are subject to inheritance tax.

- Within each tax year new investments must be made with one plan manager only. You can swap plan managers at any time but cannot split one year's allowance between two or more managers. The manager of your Single Company Pep does not have to be the same as the manager of your General Pep.

- Qualifying investments for General Peps are British and European Community shares, qualifying corporate bonds, and cash. UK-authorized unit trusts and investment trusts must have at least 50% invested in such qualifying investments in order to be eligible for Pep treatment. Where the 50% rule is not met, Pep investors may only put £1,500 per year of their £6,000 allowance into such a fund – the balance (if used) must go into qualifying investments.

  For Single Company Peps, the investment must be in the shares of a single British or European Community company share. You can change this whenever you wish but you cannot hold more than one company's shares at any one time.

  With both types of Pep, while monies may be held partially and temporarily in cash, the Revenue could withdraw tax benefits from a plan that appeared to have been kept deliberately in cash long term.

- Investors may transfer past years' Pep holdings from one plan manager to another at any time. If all their past holdings are with a single plan manager, they may have to be transferred in bulk; it depends on how the particular manager has organized its plans. Some keep holdings relating to different tax years in separate plans, in which case they can be transferred separately to a number of different managers; others lump them together in a single plan, in which case they must be transferred in bulk. Alternatively, and subject to the same provisos, investors can stick with the same plan manager but swap funds.

- Existing investments cannot be transferred directly into a

Pep; they must first be sold (and any capital gains tax paid),
then re-purchased to put into the Pep.

The place of Peps in a retirement portfolio

Peps can plan an extremely useful part in any investment portfolio
– especially in retirement because they produce tax-free income.
Anyone who has a lump sum to invest on retirement should try,
where possible, to use the Pep allowances to the maximum. While
the allowance is only £6,000 per year, remember this is doubled for
a married couple. If you are retiring a few months before the end
of a tax year, it may be worth holding back a portion of the money
until the new tax year to make use of that year's allowances; in that
way a married couple could invest up to £24,000 in the tax shelter
of a Pep over a few months.

Couples who have made maximum use of all annual Pep allowances since they were first introduced in the late 1980s could now
have a Pep portfolio well in excess of £100,000; for them, the Pep
transfer rules may be relevant as the emphasis of the portfolio
should be shifting away from growth towards the provision of
income. It should be possible to organize this shift while staying
within the Pep shelter.

Unit Trusts

Unit trusts are a pooled investment. The trust usually invests in at
least 40 different shares, and often many more; unitholders get
an appropriate slice of the whole portfolio. Like other pooled
vehicles, their main advantage is that they provide a spread of risk
which is hard to match unless you have very substantial funds of
your own. In addition, good fund managers can add considerable
value by managing the investments – although only a minority
succeed in doing so consistently.

Their disadvantage, one shared to a greater or lesser extent with
all types of share investment, is their cost. Typically, unit trusts
carry an initial charge of 5 to 5.5% and an annual management

charge of between 0.75 and 1.75%. Charges are automatically deducted from the investment. In addition to the initial charge, new investors also face the 'spread' – the difference between buying and selling prices on the shares held in the underlying portfolio. In all, this generally means there is a gap of about 6% between the amount of money you put into the trust and the amount you would get back the next day if you sold (assuming the unit price has remained constant). This gap is called the 'bid–offer spread' – 'bid' being the price at which units are bought back by the managers; 'offer' the price at which they are sold to investors. The spread may be larger than this, particularly for specialist or smaller company funds.

Many unit trust Peps have lower charges than this, though it is rare to find any trust with annual charges lower than 1 or 0.75%. However, competition has forced many managers to reduce the initial charge to 3% or even less. Some impose a 'back-end' charge on their Peps if investors cash them in within the first five years.

Unit trusts have a variety of investment objectives. Some aim to produce maximum capital growth, while disregarding income; others go for 'total return' – with profits arising from both income earned and reinvested and also capital growth; a further category – the one most likely to interest retired investors – concentrates on producing a relatively high initial level of income.

Income unit trusts: the categories
Income funds can in turn be broken down into various types. The Association of Unit Trusts and Investment Funds has the following categories:

- **UK equity income:** defined as trusts which have at least 80% of their assets in UK equities and which aim to have a yield in excess of 110% of the FTA All Share Index.
- **International equity income:** defined as trusts which invest at least 80% of their assets in equities and aim to achieve a yield in excess of 110% of the FTA World Index.
- **Balanced:** defined as trusts which invest at least 80% of their

assets in the UK, but less than 80% in either UK equities or UK fixed interest securities.
- **Convertibles:** defined as trusts which invest at least 60% of their assets in convertibles stocks (see page 114).

There are numerous other categories relating to specialist American, Japanese and emerging markets funds, but for income-seeking investors the only others of interest are likely to be the UK general category, where the yield should roughly match the All Share Index, and the gilt and fixed interest funds. Table 18 provides a summary of the current yields and average past performance over various periods for these categories. It also provides two 'benchmark' figures: the results from a building society and the performance of the All Share Index over the period.

Table 18: Unit trusts – past performance and current yields

Category	Value of £1,000 invested — years ago			Current average yield
	1	5	10	
UK equity income	1,033	1,506	3,645	4.2%
UK general	1,047	1,509	3,288	2.8%
International equity income	999	1,578	2,952	3.7%
Balanced	1,027	1,527	3,121	5.1%
Convertibles	975	1,453	2,168	6.1%
UK fixed interest	1,033	1,486	2,074	7.0%
All Share Index	1,142	1,762	3,929	3.86%
Halifax 90-day a/c	1,035	1,302	1,979	4.3%
RPI	1,035	1,182	1,570	—

Note: all figures include reinvestment of income net of basic-rate tax and are shown after deduction of the relevant charges. The current yield on the building society account relates to a £5,000 investment.

Source: Money Management (figures to 1.9.1995)

Income unit trusts: how to choose
The level of charges, the current yield and the past performance are the key criteria for choosing an income trust. Investors could

also look at when, during the year, particular trusts pay out their income.

Charges: Investors should pay particular attention to the annual management charge, because this is deducted from the income before it can be paid out. In addition, income trusts are really designed for long-term investment: someone putting their money in at age 60 could well be holding that trust for 20 years or more (assuming it remains competently managed) and, while initial charges are a pain to begin with, the effect of the annual charge makes itself felt cumulatively over time. Many income trusts (within Peps or not) have annual charges of 1% or even less; others charge 1.5% a year or more.

Yield: Current yields on UK equity income trusts vary widely from around 2% to more than 6%. The highest is not necessarily the best: a basic rule of investment is that the lower the initial yield, the greater the potential of that trust to produce a higher level of both capital and income growth. The top-performing trust over the last 10 years, for example, offers a starting yield of just 3.4% (compared to the sector's average of 4.2%); the top trust over five years has, as it happens, exactly the same yield of 3.4% – both 20% below the average.

Trusts which offer a higher than average starting yield can only achieve this in one of two ways. The first is to include in the portfolio a significant proportion of fixed interest and convertible stocks along with ordinary shares. Although these pay a higher starting income, they have little or no scope for producing growth in that income, so their long-term prospects are not so good.

The second way is to opt for higher yielding ordinary shares. But there is usually a good reason why yields on certain shares are much higher than others – the stock market has marked their prices down: it might feel the prospects of future dividend growth from that company are poor; or it might simply be that the company has fallen out of fashion or is in an unpopular sector where overall growth prospects are poor. Of course, the stock market is not always right in its assessment of companies, and sometimes the holders of such stocks do rather well as the company bounces back to health and a higher share price. But choosing such shares does inevitably mean accepting a greater level of risk.

One last point to note on the yield: the lower the target yield that fund managers have to aim for, the more stocks they can choose from. Too high a target will hamstring their decisions.

Past performance: One should obviously be wary of reading too much into past performance figures, but they should not be totally ignored. The record of the managers' ability to maintain or increase income payments over the years is especially important, and it is fair to say that some management groups appear to be able to achieve this, year after year, while others consistently fail.

Payment of dividends: Most trusts pay out dividends twice a year, although a few offer a monthly income. By constructing a small portfolio of different unit trusts, you could have income payments spread out over, say, eight months of the year. Financial advisers usually recommend that clients should not insist on a strictly monthly income, because this could mean choosing trusts solely on their payout dates rather than their underlying worth.

Index funds

There is a small but growing number of index unit trusts which are not actively managed at all, simply aiming to track the share index (either the FT-SE100 index of leading shares or the All Share Index) by a mixture of direct investment and financial derivatives contracts. Their underlying yield (before deduction of the annual fee) will match that of the index, and thus be a little lower than some high income funds. Their advantage, however, is that their charges are likely to be lower than for actively managed funds (some charge just 0.5% annual management fee) and there may thus be a place for them as a core holding in the portfolios of those who are aiming for a mixture of growth and income return.

Convertible and preference share funds

There is a handful of specialist convertible and preference share funds which might find a place in a well-spread portfolio. Preference shares are straightforward fixed interest securities, but convertibles are a halfway house between a fixed interest stock and an ordinary share: they may be converted into a company's ordinary share on fixed terms at some future date. If the company is doing well, this is a valuable option, and the convertible price will rise accordingly. Convertibles have been described as offering an equity 'kicker' to a fixed interest stock.

Most of these funds may now be put into a Pep, and the average yield stands at around 6%.

Investment Trusts

Investment trusts are pooled investments designed, like unit trusts, to provide a spread of risk for those with relatively small amounts to invest. However, unlike unit trusts, they are actually limited companies themselves, quoted on the Stock Exchange. The 'split-capital' trusts described in the previous chapter (see page 101 have a redemption date – the date at which the trust will be wound down and the proceeds of the investment distributed to its shareholders in the manner laid down in its constitution. Most trusts, however, are set up to last indefinitely.

Some of these trusts are venerable beings: the oldest, Foreign and Colonial, was set up in the 1850s, and many of the other big, general trusts were incorporated before the end of the last century. Others have been formed in the last decade.

There are two essential differences between unit and investment trusts from the investor's point of view. Firstly, investment trust companies are allowed to borrow. Managers are likely to do this if they think the prospects for the stock market they are investing in are so good that the exercise will yield them a profit even after paying interest on the borrowed money. If the managers are right, this 'gearing', as it is called, is good news for the investors; if they are wrong, investors will be in a worse position than if their trust had no gearing at all.

Secondly, investment trusts are quoted companies, which means that their share prices are influenced not just by the value of their underlying investments, but also by the levels of supply and demand for the trusts' shares themselves. Throughout the 1970s and the early 1980s investment trusts were deeply unfashionable. Plenty of people wanted to sell them; no one much wanted to buy. As a result, their share price was often at a significant discount to their net asset value – perhaps 25% or more – and it would have paid shareholders then to see the trust broken up and the assets distributed. But trusts have recently become much more popular, and in most cases the discount has largely disappeared. People who bought back in the 70s and early 80s have since done handsomely from their investment, because they experienced 'windfall' gains as the discount narrowed and trusts' share prices rose over and above the gain in their underlying portfolios.

These days the opposite phenomenon is now appearing: trusts whose share price stands at a premium to their net asset value. Too high a premium is dangerous, because sooner or later it will be likely to fall back to net asset value, providing their investors with what is, in effect, a windfall loss.

Investment trusts: how to choose

The Association of Investment Trust Companies provides a raft of useful explanatory literature on how trusts work and their past performance, along with details of current discounts or premiums and the level of gearing for each trust. Investors should have a careful look at these statistics: an above-average gearing factor means a riskier investment, while a trust standing at a large premium to its net asset value is also to be avoided.

Many firms of private client stockbrokers will offer advice on investment trusts, and there is much to be said for seeking it, given the extra complexities of the vehicle compared to unit trusts. However, there is nothing to stop anyone choosing for themselves. Most trusts run special investment schemes for private investors and charge relatively low fees for purchases and sales. Where trusts qualify as eligible investments under the Pep rules, investors can usually invest via a Pep at no extra charge. In addition to the costs of buying, all trusts have an annual management charge. Generally speaking, annual fees are lower for investment trusts than for unit trusts.

Unit and Investment Trusts: the Tax Position

Investments made through a Personal Equity Plan are not liable to income or capital gains tax. Otherwise income is paid net of a 20% tax charge: basic-rate taxpayers have no further liability, but higher-rate taxpayers must declare the income and pay an additional 20% tax. Capital gains realized within the trusts attract no tax; however, when investors sell their holdings, they are potentially liable to capital gains tax on any profits made, although of course they can use their annual CGT exemption (currently £6,300) to set against these profits. This makes unit and investment trusts on the whole a more attractive proposition than life assurance single premium bonds (see below).

Life Assurance Bonds

Single premium life assurance linked bonds are a third form of pooled investment aimed at the private investor. Like the others, they provide a spread of risk and professional investment management; their charges are similar to those of unit trusts, or a little lower.

The main difference lies in their tax treatment. Bonds come under the tax regime for life company investments, and the main consequences are as follows:

- Income arising within a bond is taxed at the basic-rate, which cannot be reclaimed by non-taxpayers. Higher-rate taxpayers do not face any immediate further charge, but see below.
- Up to 5% of the bond's original value may be withdrawn by investors for a period of 20 years, free of tax. This counts as return of capital. This allowance can be carried over so that, if nothing is withdrawn during the first 10 years, a total of 10% may be withdrawn for the following 10 years. Any withdrawals above this limit are free of tax for basic-rate taxpayers, but attract an additional tax charge in the hands of higher-rate taxpayers.
- Capital gains realized within the bond are taxed at 25%, which is automatically deducted from the value of the holdings. Holders cannot use their own annual CGT exemption to set against these gains.
- When the bond is sold, basic-rate taxpayers have nothing further to pay. Higher-rate taxpayers face a further 16% charge on the profits. To establish the extent of this liability the proceeds from the sale are added to any earlier 5% withdrawals. The original purchase price is then deducted from the total, and the resulting amount – in effect, the total profit (whether derived from reinvested income or capital gains) – is divided by the number of years the investor has held the bond. That sum is then added to the investor's income for the year in question, to establish whether it would give rise to a higher-rate tax liability. If it does, then the whole of the profit is taxed at higher-rate minus basic-rate – in other words, 40% minus 24%, or 16%.

This rather complicated procedure is known as 'top-slicing'. Overall, bonds are more heavily taxed than unit or investment trusts, whether for basic- or higher-rate taxpayers, especially where the underlying investments of the bond are such that much of the total profit has come from capital gains rather than the reinvestment of income.

However, the 'top-slicing' formula has one beneficial effect where people are able to arrange their income. For instance, a self-employed higher-rate taxpayer on the point of retirement might be able to defer taking all, or much, of his pension in the first year, and use that year to encash his bonds. Assuming he has no other large sources of taxable income, the profits could be free of any additional tax.

A word of warning: this whole system of taxing life assurance bonds is under review at the moment, and changes may well be made during 1996 which make them less attractive to anyone near the higher-rate threshold.

Investing in Shares Directly

Many investors prefer to invest directly in company shares rather than through the medium of one of the pooled investment vehicles. Given the need to spread risk among a number of different companies, the minimum investment required to make this a sensible move is around £50,000 – some brokers would say much more.

Investing directly does not, of course, mean going without the tax advantages of Peps. Many stockbrokers run 'share-only' Personal Equity Plans where, for an additional fee, investors can benefit from the Pep's tax freedoms. These fees do vary, but they are not always cheaper than unit trust or investment trust Peps. If you are considering this route, it may be worth getting hold of an annual publication called *PepGuide*, which lists the plans available and their charges (see Appendix 1, page 163).

Single Company Peps

Finally, investors with significant assets have probably already been using their £3,000 annual allowance for Single Company Peps. In one sense, they fly in the face of all investment theory, offering absolutely no spread of risk. But, of course, you can choose a different share each year for your SCP, and as long as they form only a part of an overall portfolio, there is much to be said for making sure you make maximum use of this tax exemption as well.

11 | *Investment Planning in Practice*

Investors should treat this chapter with some caution. Its purpose is not to tell you precisely where you should be putting your money now, but simply to provide an idea of the sort of portfolio that you probably ought to have at retirement. At any given point in time there is, of course, no single answer to this question because so much depends on you, the investor: how much you have to invest, the size of your pension and your liabilities, and your general attitude to investment.

To this range of variables one could add countless others: do you intend to move house now or later? Are you retiring in your early 50s or late 60s? Do you want to leave significant sums to your children? Do you expect to be beneficiaries from the estates of your parents or other relatives?

All these factors should be taken into account by a competent financial adviser. Only after assessing all of them would he or she then suggest an investment portfolio, based on investment conditions prevailing at that time. Despite all these caveats, however, it seems a worthwhile exercise to attempt to put some flesh on the bones of the generalizations that this book has described hitherto. And it is fair to say that, although the details will inevitably be different, if your circumstances are something like any of the five examples given below, then the structure of your portfolio ought to be something like the appropriate solutions described.

The Characteristics of a Good Portfolio

If you decide to undergo a similar exercise yourself, then it is worth taking one step back from the final recommendations and asking the following questions:

- Does it meet all your needs?
- If not, does it meet the most important needs, and are the reasons why they cannot all be met sensible ones?
- Does it match with your risk profile? – in other words, are you happy with the level of risk the portfolio involves?
- Does it build in enough flexibility to cope at least with minor emergencies?
- Does it ensure you have enough liquid funds?
- Does it involve a proper spread of risk?
- Will it take care of longer term requirements as well as the immediate future?

If you are happy in your own mind with the answers to all these questions, then that is the hallmark of a job well done.

The following 'solutions' have been provided by a number of different independent financial advisers and stockbrokers.

Example One

The problem
Arthur Clough, aged 62, is retiring on a company pension of £14,000 from a medium-sized company operating a final salary pension scheme. His wife, Mary, is 59. The scheme has lately been paying out inflation-matching increases to pensioners but this has been on an ex gratia basis.

He can either take the full pension or tax-free cash of £33,000, which will provide a reduced pension of £10,500. Mary gave up her job a year ago, and has no pension entitlement other than the basic State pension, which will provide slightly more on her own record (£1,998 per year) than by claiming on her husband's.

They are good money-managers but cautious by nature and a little worried about how they will manage in retirement. They own their home and would like, eventually, to leave 'something' to the children but, since both are happily settled and in good jobs, see no need to make any special plans for doing so. Their other investments are:

£17,000 in various building society accounts
£5,000 in a Tessa (with two years to run to completion)
around £2,400 in various privatizations – split equally between BT, British Gas and TSB.

Their only immediate spending plans are 'a good holiday' costing up to £2,000. Should they take the lump sum? If so, where should they invest it?

A solution
Provided by Danby Bloch of Raymond Godfrey and Partners, a firm of independent financial advisers.

The tax-free lump sum available from a pension scheme is often one of its most attractive elements, but Arthur and Mary need to think very carefully before they decide to take it. If they do opt for the cash, they are giving up a pension of £3,500 a year.

The main problem lies in deciding whether Arthur's company will continue paying out increases on the pension to match inflation. Even if the increases only partially meet inflation, that still means giving up a valuable benefit. Investing £33,000 in a building society would only provide a gross yearly income of about £2,300 – at best – at current interest rates and, assuming all the income was withdrawn, there would be no scope for future growth. An index-linked annuity providing a yearly gross income of £3,500 would cost a great deal more than £33,000 to buy.

If, on the other hand, it is very unlikely that his company will pay out any increases at all in future, the couple might consider taking the cash sum and investing it – but the chances are they would still be better off in the long term sticking to the full pension.

If they are nevertheless determined to take the cash, and they want a long-term, growing income, then income unit trusts could be at least part of the answer. Over the years these investments have generally provided steadily growing income as well as attractive capital growth. As much as possible of these trusts should be held within Peps so that both income and growth will be tax-free.

Because the pension counts as Arthur's income for tax purposes, taxable investments should be held in Mary's name, so that she can make use of the balance of her personal allowance. Their other investments should include enough cash in a building society to meet unexpected needs, perhaps £5,000 to £10,000. Some of this could be held in Tessas: if they do not in fact need to withdraw capital within the five-year term, they will then benefit from the tax exemption.

Although Mary gave up work last year, she could still make a single premium contribution to a personal pension plan and relate that back to last year. She would get immediate tax relief of 25%, and could start drawing the income at once – or leave it until she needs it.

Example Two

The problem

Thomas Gray is a self-employed man, and decides to retire at the age of 66. His wife Vivien is four years younger. He has built up a total pension fund of £78,000, of which £20,000 is in a RAP and the rest in a personal pension. His options are to take a level pension of £8,000 (including a widow's pension of 50%) or one of £6,200 increasing at 3% a year. Alternatively, he can take a cash sum of approximately £20,000 and a reduced pension of £6,400 (level) or £5,100 (increasing at 3%). Because he has not yet drawn his basic old age pension, he merits a 7.5% increase in the amount payable, bringing it to approximately £5,280.

His only other investments are:

£22,000 in various building society accounts (held in his name)
£5,000 of Vivien's, held in accounts in her name, where she gets the interest paid gross

*a Tessa, which is due to mature in the next few months, paying out
£10,200
a life assurance-linked managed bond, currently worth £6,800.*

*Thomas and Vivien would like to have a total income of £800 a
month after tax but could manage on less. They need to replace their
car shortly and are mentally setting aside £5,000 (perhaps from the
proceeds of the Tessa) to do so. What sort of pension should they
take – and where should their money be invested?*

A solution

Provided by Amanda Davidson of Holden Meehan, a firm of
independent financial advisers.

*The biggest threat for any investment portfolio is not short-term
volatility but long-term inflation. So Thomas and Vivien should
take the tax-free cash of £20,000 and opt for a pension increasing at
3% a year, which will start at £5,100 a year. This includes a widow's
pension of 50% – an important point, as Vivien does not appear to
have a pension income of her own.*

*The State and personal pensions between them should provide a
net monthly income of £795, thus more or less meeting the Grays'
target figure, though it would be wise to aim for a little more –
perhaps an extra £50 a month – to cover emergencies. This can be
achieved by using part of the tax-free cash to invest back into a
personal pension. Under the carry-back and carry-forward tax
rules, Arthur can back-track over seven previous years to pick
up previously unused entitlements to invest in his pension. By
using £12,000 of his cash sum to do so, he is entitled to tax relief on
that sum at the basic rate of tax, bringing the net cost down to
£9,120.*

*Further, he can take a quarter of the total investment (£3,000) as a
cash sum, bringing the cost down to a little over £6,000. This
pension fund will at current rates buy him a pension of almost £800
a year (again, increasing at 3% a year).*

It might seem strange to use some of the pension cash to invest in a pension, but it is perfectly legitimate, so long as Arthur has sufficient 'net relevant earnings' from previous years to do so. Given that for the last five years he has been allowed to put up to 40% of his net relevant earnings into a pension, this is highly likely – very few people manage to save such a big proportion of their income.

Having sorted out the income question, we now have a freer hand as regards the rest of the Grays' investments. They have a total of £51,000 made up of: building societies – £27,000 in total; pension cash – £14,000 in total; Tessa – £10,200. In addition to this there is the £6,800 managed bond. The money should be invested as follows:

Amount	Investment	Name
£5,000	'Car money' held in building society	Vivien
£5,000	Building society	Vivien
£5,000	NS 8th issue index-linked certificates	Arthur
£6,000	Peps	Arthur
£30,000	Unit trusts	either Vivien or jointly
£6,800	Managed bond	Arthur

Building society investments: Some money must be set aside for emergencies, and should be held in Vivien's name, along with the car money, so that she can get the interest gross. There is little point in their reinvesting in a further Tessa.

National Savings Certificates: The 8th index-linked issue provides 3% over retail price inflation, guaranteed for five years and tax-free, making it a suitable and secure investment, and a good hedge should inflation rise markedly.

Peps and unit trusts: These investments are set aside to provide capital growth with a view to providing income in the future – essential if inflation exceeds the annual 3% rate at which Arthur's personal pension is increasing. The Pep, being tax-free, should be in his name; the rest can be held either jointly or in Vivien's name. The unit trusts should be split as follows: 40% in the UK, 20% in

Europe, 10% in the US, 10% in the Far East and 20% in general international funds. They should be growth-oriented trusts, providing little in the way of income now, but may be switched later to income-producing investments. These are long-term investments and should be held for five years plus.

The managed bond: This is not an ideal investment from a tax point of view; however, if they are happy with its past performance, they might as well keep it; if it has not done so well, however, they could cash it in now and add the proceeds to their unit trust portfolio.

Overall, the Grays have, for the present time, a comfortable income to live on, which means they can afford to look ahead, and to take on board some risk with a view to securing capital growth potential for the future, by means of a good, well-balanced portfolio of equities.

Example Three

The problem
George Herbert retires at 61 with a company pension of £25,000 a year and a cash sum of £80,000. He and his wife Anne (aged 58) have a reasonably extensive investment portfolio, built up somewhat haphazardly over the years. Between them, they have:

£40,000 in growth-oriented Peps, largely invested in the UK, although £10,000 is in European funds
Nearly £18,000 in Tessas (due for maturity in a few months' time)
£30,000 in building societies, in Anne's name
£8,000 in a high-interest cheque account – the proceeds of an endowment policy which they have yet to decide where to reinvest
£4,000 in Japanese unit trusts

They would like an additional £5,000 or more investment income to spend, but are very keen to retain potential for growth. At present they live in a large house worth perhaps £200,000, which is fairly expensive to run. They anticipate moving at some stage, but have formed no definite plans. They would like to be able to leave reasonably substantial funds to their children.

They have decided to take the lump sum and have earmarked £10,000 of this for various immediate spending plans. Where should they invest the rest to meet their needs?

A solution

Provided by Peter Hargreaves of Hargreaves Lansdown, a firm of independent financial advisers.

George and Anne will have total capital of around £180,000 to invest once they retire, less the £10,000 required for short-term spending. Their existing portfolio is quite well spread, but a shift in emphasis away from growth towards income will help to provide the extra income they require. A total of £12,000 from their liquid capital should be reserved for next year's Pep entitlements, and this should be invested in corporate bond Peps, while £10,000 of their existing growth Peps should be switched into the same investments. The remaining £20,000 of UK growth Peps should be switched to UK equity income Peps, and perhaps in due course the European Peps could be similarly transferred – it will depend on the couple's future needs for income.

Meanwhile, Anne should continue holding her £30,000 in a building society for the time being, together with £8,000 in the high-interest cheque account. A total of £40,000 from the cash sum should be placed in a portfolio of equity income funds in Anne's name – and the total income from these three sources should use her tax-free personal allowance in full.

The Tessas should be retained and, once matured, should be converted in Tessas Mark Two to retain the tax advantages. Finally, the remainder of the cash available for investment, £18,000, should be placed in a small portfolio of growth-oriented unit and investment trusts (together with the existing £4,000), investing in Japan, the emerging markets, America and the Far East. This should generate capital growth and provide the means to invest in Peps in later years, perhaps with a switch to income-producing investments, depending on whether the couple feel the need for extra income at that stage. This portfolio, which will produce very little if any income immediately, may be held in George's name.

As regards inheritance tax, the couple are really too young as yet to consider serious moves to plan for this, although they might consider starting a whole of life assurance policy written in absolute trust for the children, which would provide an immediate cash sum to meet all, or a part of, any future tax liability.

Overall, as the schedule shows, this investment portfolio produces a good level of income (in excess of £7,000 a year), most of which will be free of tax. More importantly, £60,000 of the total is committed to equity income funds, which should provide both a growing income and some prospects of capital growth over the years, while a further £22,000 is also in equities.

Investment	Amount	Income
Anne's portfolio		
Tessa	£9,000	£630
Building society	£30,000	£1,800
High interest cheque account	£8,000	£125
European Pep	£5,000	Nil
Corporate bond Pep	£11,000	£880
Equity income Pep	£10,000	£400
Equity income funds	£40,000	£1,600
George's portfolio		
Tessa	£9,000	£630
European Pep	£5,000	Nil
Corporate bond Pep	£11,000	£880
Equity income Pep	£10,000	£400
Growth portfolio	£22,000	Nil
	£170,000	**£7,345**

Example Four

The problem
Liz Barrett, aged 60, retires after many years as personal assistant to the managing director of a small manufacturing and exporting company, on a final salary of nearly £20,000. For much of her career she made no pension savings, but in the last 10 years has been putting money into a personal pension, into which her company has been making contributions as well.

The fund is now worth £44,000. She has her own flat which is fully paid for; however, the service charges have shown a worrying tendency to increase well above inflation in the last few years. Having helped her company in the struggle to remain competitive in world markets through the raging inflation of the 1970s and 1980s, Liz is very conscious of the need for protection against future inflation.

In addition to her pension savings, she has £18,000 in building society accounts, mostly at short notice. She will qualify for the full single person's old age pension and has some Serps entitlement as well. Her pension fund will buy her a pension of approximately £4,100 on a level basis, but just £2,400 if she opts for an index-linked pension, and she would ideally prefer a little more. What should she do?

A solution
Provided by Vanessa Barnes of Chase de Vere Investments, a firm of independent financial advisers.

At least the first slice of Liz's retirement income, the State pension, will be fully protected against inflation, so it is perhaps not so critical that her personal pension be completely index-linked. At current rates, and assuming average inflation of 5% in the future, it would take 13 years for the lower starting rate of an index-linked pension to catch up with the level of a flat rate pension. Instead, Liz might like to consider a personal pension increasing at a fixed rate of 3% a year. At current annuity rates, her £44,000 would buy a pension of £3,115 with 3% escalation.

As an alternative, Liz could also consider taking the maximum tax-free cash sum of £11,000 and a commensurately reduced pension. Because the State pension will use up all her tax-free personal allowance, her personal pension will be fully taxed, so taking the cash and investing it in tax-free vehicles such as Tessas and Peps has something to recommend it.

Together with her current building society deposits, she has a total of £29,000 available for investment. She could place £3,000 in a Tessa immediately, and the balance of £7,000 in an instant access postal account. Once she is sure of how her budget pans out, she could transfer extra sums into the Tessa in subsequent years, depending on whether or not she feels happy with locking up the cash effectively for five years in the Tessa.

A further £5,000 should go into index-linked National Savings Certificates. These have the advantage of growing at an interest rate above inflation. Although there will be no income initially, after the five-year term the increased capital will be available and might be 'earmarked' for future service fees.

She should consider an equity income Pep to provide a growing income tax-free as well as potential capital growth. The sum of £6,000 could be invested in a Pep this year, and a further £6,000 could be put into an equity income trust, and switched into a Pep in a year's time, when her new Pep allowance becomes available. In order to minimize risk, one of these Peps could have a proportion of gilts or other fixed interest investments in its portfolio.

Finally, although Liz would appear to be a relatively conservative investor, she has experienced the benefit of equity growth via her pension fund and particularly through her former employer's business. So she might be happy to think about investing the remaining £2,000 in a unit trust concentrating on growth from companies in the UK or, perhaps, diversify into the emerging markets. Although unlikely to provide much in the way of an immediate income, the potential capital gain would provide protection against long-term inflation – although she would have to accept that this type of fund carries a higher risk profile.

Investment	Amount	Net income p.a.
Tessa	£3,000	£160
Building society postal account	£7,000	£313
NS index-linked certificates	£5,000	Nil
High income Pep	£6,000	£240
Extra income unit trust	£6,000	£240
International emerging markets trust	£2,000	Nil
	£29,000	**£953**

Example Five

The problem
Christopher Smart, a partner in a firm of management consultants, has decided to retire two years early at the age of 58. He has personal pension funds totalling £400,000. His wife Jane, three years younger, works part time in an art gallery and has no intention of stopping work for the time being. Her income is relatively low – about £8,000 a year – and is, in any case, 'hers' – not to be taken into account in his own planning.

In addition to the pension fund, the couple have an equity portfolio currently worth £168,000. Much of it was inherited from Christopher's mother, who died three years ago, and represents a collection of shares, unit and investment trusts built up by his father over the years. He admits the portfolio could probably do with an overhaul and would like an adviser to recommend an 'ideal' portfolio, which he could then compare with what he actually has, making such changes as he sees fit. £30,000 of the total is in various Personal Equity Plans, but he has not done one this year.

While he is formally retiring, Christopher expects to be doing some consulting work during the next few years on an ad hoc basis – indeed, he is currently discussing a possible project which is likely to come to fruition in about nine months' time and could be very remunerative for him (though unlikely to last for more than about a year). Meanwhile, he needs income – he reckons, about £2,000 a month after tax – but with flexibility as well.

The couple have Tessas totalling £18,000 and liquid funds in building societies of approximately £47,000. They would like to keep this – whether it is tax efficient or not – because they have recently acquired a 'cowshed' in France which requires extensive modernization.

A solution

Provided by Michael Otway of stockbrokers Carr Sheppards.

Christopher has two main immediate requirements: a net income of about £2,000 a month, and the flexibility to vary this so that, if his consultancy work comes to fruition, he does not end up with 'unwanted' income on which he may have to pay tax at a high rate.

For this reason it is not a good idea for Christopher to buy a pension annuity straight away with his pension fund. He is relatively young, and must plan ahead for a life expectancy of some 30 years. Instead, he should take out a managed pension and use the drawdown facility. At his age, the minimum pension income that must be withdrawn is 3.43% of the pension fund; the maximum is 9.8%.

Christopher should take the maximum tax-free cash, in other words £100,000 (25% × £400,000), which will be invested with the rest of his portfolio. Then, in his first year of retirement, he could take 6% of the remaining fund, giving a gross income of £18,000. In year two, if he has consultancy earnings, he can reduce the drawdown to 3.43% and keep it there during year three. There is then a compulsory review and the minimum will rise to 3.68%. What he should take at that point will depend on his circumstances then.

At this stage, he should obtain a forecast of his State pension entitlements by filling out form BR19, and should probably continue paying National Insurance Contributions on a voluntary basis for the next two years (after age 60 they will be credited free) to maximize his entitlement to State benefits.

The building society accounts and Tessas will be left undisturbed, to enable the couple to carry out renovation work on their 'cow-

shed'. If possible, once the Tessas have matured, the full amount allowable (£9,000 from each Tessa) should be rolled over into the Tessa Mark Two, to allow the tax exemptions to continue.

The rest of their investments now total £30,000 in Peps, and £238,000 of which £100,000 is in cash awaiting investment. This needs to be discussed in more detail with Christopher and Jane in order to establish their investment aims and attitudes to risk, but the following are the general principles that should operate:

The portfolio should be split as follows: 35% in fixed interest investments and 65% in asset-backed investments such as property or (preferably) shares. To achieve this split, £60,000 of the cash should be invested in fixed interest investments which may include, for example, cash deposits, National Savings Certificates, gilts and corporate bonds, the precise mix depending on their need for income.

The ownership of the existing portfolio needs to be reviewed to make sure that both partners can make full use of their basic-rate tax bands, and avoid a situation where one may be paying 40% tax on income, while the other has not exhausted the basic-rate entitlement. To do this means putting most of the investments in Jane's name.

Both partners should make full use of this year's annual Pep allowances: this means a total of £18,000, as each can invest £6,000 in a General Pep and £3,000 in a Single Company Pep. The remaining £22,000 from the £100,000 cash will be invested alongside the existing portfolio. Their long-term aim should be to use the allowances each year to shift as much as possible of the investment portfolio into Peps.

£60,000: fixed interest – gilts, quality preference shares plus some zero-dividend preference shares

£50,000: overseas investments, including Japan, US, European and emerging markets, via unit and investment trusts

£40,000: UK smaller companies and other specialist areas, via unit and investment trusts

£118,000: a spread of blue chip UK shares.

Summary of assets and income

	Christopher investment	Income (gross)	Jane investment	Income (gross)
Assets				
House and contents	£120,000	—	£120,000	—
Cowshed	£5,000	—	£5,000	—
Tessa	£9,000	—	£9,000	—
Building society	£23,000	£1,175	£23,500	£1,175
Peps	£39,000	£1,950	£9,000	£450
Fixed interest	—	—	£60,000	£3,600
Equities (incl. trusts)	—	—	£160,000	£5,600
Earnings				
Personal pension	£18,000			—
Income from work	—			£8,000
Total income before tax		£21,125		£18,825
Total income after tax		**£17,898**		**£15,890**

Notes: It is assumed the building society investments produce 5% gross and the Peps 5% tax-free. The equity portfolio overall is assumed to yield 3.5% gross and the fixed interest portfolio, 6% gross. The total spendable income of £33,788 will provide Christopher with just over £2,200 per month, which will meet his requirements, while Jane retains approximately £7,140 net per year from her gross earnings of £8,000.

12 | *Financial Planning for the Fourth Age*

Investments that suit people in their late 50s will not necessarily be appropriate for those in their 70s or 80s. A well-constructed portfolio of investments should be resilient enough to cope with the damage inflicted by inflation over the years, but a major part of an investor's total retirement income may fail to provide such protection. In particular, those who had to arrange their own pension annuities (the self-employed, for example), and who opted for the highest level of immediate income at the outset, will have been living on a fixed income ever since, and although their State pension will have risen in line with prices in the meantime, this will not necessarily compensate for the fall-off in purchasing power of the rest of their pension.

In any case, there comes a time when some of the words that trip off a financial adviser's tongue, such as 'going for long-term growth', seem rather less relevant than they might have done 20 years earlier. All in all, there is a case to be made for retirement planning to be done in two stages: around the time of retirement itself, and then perhaps 10 or 15 years later, as people settle into their mid-70s.

Peps

Financial planning for what might be called 'the fourth age' has been made a great deal easier by the introduction of Peps. Until they came along, investors were in an awkward position: the most tax-efficient way to obtain regular payouts from their investments was, in fact, to realize capital gains each year, because investors could utilize their annual exemption of £6,000-odd and obtain such money tax-free; income, on the other hand, would be taxed immediately – and those whose income was caught in the 'age allowance trap' (see the next chapter, page 144), found themselves paying a very high tax bill.

But many people in their 70s or 80s do not really want to deal with the sort of higher-risk portfolio likely to produce such gains, nor indeed to undergo the annual hassle of deciding what to sell. Peps have done away with the need for all that, because both income and gains from Peps are tax-free. The best way to prepare now for financial planning in later life is to make sure that as much of your portfolio as possible is held within Peps.

Once within the structure of the Pep, remember, funds can be switched from one type of investment to another without losing the tax advantages, so it is a good idea to switch funds from equity Peps into corporate bond Peps. The switch does not have to be made in one go – on your 75th birthday, for example – but could be phased in over a number of years. At current yields, a switch from a general equity Pep to a bond Pep could result in a doubling of income, from around 3 or 4% to 7.5 or 8%. While the actual figures might change, unless the world turns upside down between now and then, one can expect this kind of increase.

If you do decide to switch bit by bit, make sure that your current Peps are held in separate accounts: you can either have a clutch of different managers, or choose a Pep manager who does not lump all Pep holdings into a single account (in which case they must then be switched in a lump or not at all).

Avoiding Inheritance Tax

If you have not done so already, this reorganization of your portfolio could well prompt you to consider making some practical moves to help your ultimate heirs avoid inheritance tax (IHT). This is a complicated subject and is dealt with more fully in Chapter 13 (see page 152), but it is worth noting here that certain types of investment – those which produce high income but involve the diminution of capital – can be positively beneficial when seen in the light of IHT. One of the simplest ways to escape IHT is to give away money while you are alive. This is all very well in theory, but people generally need their capital in order to provide an income. Suppose, however, you could produce the same level of income with only half or two-thirds of the capital, then it might be possible to give away the rest.

That could be achieved by buying an ordinary life annuity (see Chapter 5, page 55), but do look at how their rates – and more particularly, the net rates after tax – rise with age. An annuity of any sort involves handing over your capital irrevocably to a life company and in return getting a fixed income guaranteed to last the rest of your life (however long or short that might be). Because life expectancy falls with age, the rates available rise.

But, in addition, a life annuity (as opposed to a pension annuity) is taxed in a peculiar way: a certain proportion of each payment counts as 'return of capital' and is tax-free. This proportion (which is fixed by the Inland Revenue) also rises with age. The table shown on page 62 illustrated the level of capital content for various ages up to age 75; the figures in Table 19 show how it continues to rise. The balance of the annuity payment, the interest portion, is taxable. For basic-rate taxpayers, the interest is taxed at 20% and they have no further liability. Higher-rate taxpayers must pay an additional 20% on this portion. Pension annuities, by contrast, are taxed as if they were earnings – in other words, basic-rate tax-payers have to pay the full rate (currently 24%) on the whole of the pension annuity payment.

Remember that all annuity payments depend on the level of interest rates at the time the annuity was purchased, so if you are buying one when rates are lower than at the time of writing, the annuity payments will also be lower than those shown in Table 19.

Whether or not inheritance tax planning plays a part in all this, it is clear that buying an ordinary annuity will immediately increase

Table 19: Ordinary annuities at older ages

1. Amount of tax-free capital content per year on payments produced by a £10,000 purchase price.

Man aged 75	£911	Woman aged 75	£771
Man aged 80	£1,195	Woman aged 80	£1,025
Man aged 85	£1,614	Woman aged 85	£1,410
Joint man 78/woman 75	£663		

2. Annual annuity payments, net of basic-rate tax for purchase price of £10,000

Annuitant	Payment	Annuitant	Payment
Man 75	£1,445	Woman 75	£1,219
Man 80	£1,798	Woman 80	£1,510
Man 85	£2,309	Woman 85	£1,959
Joint 78/75	£1,080		

The joint annuity lasts until the second death. Payments are made monthly in arrears, with no guaranteed period.

Source: Annuity Direct

your income. The price is giving up your capital; but the security is knowing that the income will last throughout the rest of your life.

There are other investments, too, which have annuity-like characteristics. For example, high coupon gilts, dealt with in Chapter 8 (see page 92), can produce an income above the going rate, at the price of an eventual loss in capital value. To take an extreme example, at the time of writing Treasury 13.5% 2004–8 has a running yield (in other words, the yield actually receivable by its holders) of 10.18% gross – this at a time when building society rates are around 5 to 7% gross – but it costs £132.66 to buy £100 of stock. That means a £32.66 loss on redemption which will take place sometime between 2004 and 2008. But a nonagenarian buying in 1995 may not be too concerned about this loss. However, care needs to be taken with gilts, because all the income is taxable.

Income shares from split level investment trusts should also be considered by investors who place income needs above capital preservation (see Chapter 9, page 101). What makes them different from gilts or annuities is that the income, although high, actually comes from share dividends, which means it should continue to grow over the years, keeping pace more or less with inflation and perhaps doing rather better. However, these are specialist vehicles and you should seek professional advice, probably from a stockbroker.

Using Your Home as Income

Many people are, in terms of total assets, considered 'rich' – and yet find it hard to make ends meet on a day-to-day basis. Despite the recent fall in property values, many retired people today are living in houses worth perhaps £100,000, £200,000 or even more, which they own outright; but, of course, because they live there, they cannot realize that money to live on.

This is where the various types of home income plan may have a useful role to play. None of the schemes is a perfect answer to the dilemma of the 'asset rich/cash poor', and they should be considered alongside the alternative of selling up and moving to a smaller place, which could release significant amounts of capital and carry the bonus of lower running costs.

Nevertheless, this answer is not going to appeal to everyone. So what can home income plans provide? There are two basic types of scheme; both are 'safe' in the sense that they will not land homeowners with unexpected debts nor depend on investments performing well. Readers may remember a financial scandal in the early 1990s involving certain types of home income plan which landed thousands of pensioners with huge debts and, in some cases, cost them their homes before the authorities stepped in to put matters right. The schemes now available are quite different, and although they have disadvantages, these are clear at the outset, as are the guarantees they provide.

Home income plan 1

The basic scheme involves taking out a mortgage on the property for up to £30,000. The cash raised is then used to buy an annuity which pays out an income for life. Part of the income is used to pay the interest on the loan, while the balance belongs to the home-owner. The Government allows mortgage interest tax relief at the full basic rate of tax to be set against the interest (unlike ordinary homebuyers, where relief has been cut to 15%). Both the annuity rate and the loan rate are fixed for life so there is absolutely no danger of any drop in the net income receivable. The capital owing on the mortgage is only paid off when the property is sold – generally, after the death of the planholder, although you could sell during your lifetime (perhaps to move into sheltered accommodation), in which case the loan must be paid off then – and you will be left with the (increased) annuity payments for life.

The main drawback with this scheme is that the figures only start to make sense for people well into their 70s; at earlier ages, annuity rates are too low. The rule of thumb is that single people should be aged at least 70; with married couples, their joint ages should total a minimum of 145 or 150. The older you are at outset, the higher your income will be. Because annuities cease to be paid on the planholder's death, it may be worth considering a variation on the scheme, which offers some capital protection if the holder were to die shortly after the plan is taken out, although this does mean a lower level of income.

Of course, taking out such a plan means that there will be less money available to leave to heirs, as the capital must be repaid on death, so it may not be attractive to those wanting to leave their house to someone else to live in (although it would be preferable to home income plan 2). Because the loan is for a fixed value, any future growth in the property value belongs to the homeowner.

Home income plan 2

The second type of scheme, also known as a 'home reversion plan', provides a higher income but involves selling the whole, or a portion of, the property outright. Planholders retain the right to stay in the property as long as they live – generally for the payment of a nominal rent of perhaps £1 a month – and they continue to be responsible for the upkeep and repairs to the property.

The price paid for a property under a reversion plan is much lower than its current market value. It depends partly on age (the younger you are, the lower it is) but is unlikely to be much above half the current market value. The proceeds may be taken either as a lump sum, or an income for life, or perhaps a mixture of the two.

Home reversion schemes offer a higher level of income than the other type of scheme, and consequently are viable at younger ages – from around 65. Their disadvantages are obvious: your home is no longer your own, any future growth belongs to the life company and there is, of course, nothing to leave to your heirs.

Table 20 gives some examples of the levels of income that were available from each of these schemes at the end of 1995. New tax rates operative from April 1996 will change these figures but the difference is unlikely to be significant.

Whichever scheme you might have in mind, it is obviously sensible to think carefully before going ahead, and perhaps discuss it with your children first – certainly with your solicitor.

Eligibility for State benefits

One important factor to take into account is whether the extra income or capital sum would affect your eligibility for various State benefits such as Income Support and Council Tax benefits. The Citizen's Advice Bureau may well be able to advise on this aspect.

Home income plans and inheritance tax (IHT)

A home income plan can help reduce the eventual inheritance tax bill paid by your heirs, so the capital loss involved in taking one out may be smaller than it appears. If the total value of your estate is above the IHT nil rate band (£154,000 for the 1995–96 tax year and £200,000 from April 1996), the excess is taxed at 40%.

Table 20: Annual income available from home income and home reversion plans

(a) Home income plans
Income after payment of loan interest, assuming £30,000 loan

Age	Woman		Man		Age	Couple	
	Gross	Net	Gross	Net		Gross	Net
70	£1,006	£738	£1,639	£1,296	W72/M73	£849	£589
75	£1,469	£1,213	£2,203	£1,866	Both 75	£1,103	£766
80	£2,088	£1,864	£3,168	£2,799	Both 80	£1,425	£1,212

Note: income figures do not provide any capital protection.

(b) Home reversion plans
Assuming the property is worth £60,000 and the homeowner sells three-quarters of it

Cash available

Age	Woman	Man	Age	Couple
70	£18,580	£19,670	Both 70	£17,580
75	£21,050	£22,070	Both 75	£20,080
80	£22,750	£23,150	Both 80	£22,290

Or income for life

Age	Woman	Man	Age	Couple
70	£1,609	£2,188	Both 70	£1,133
75	£2,245	£2,975	Both 75	£1,659
80	£3,090	£3,960	Both 80	£2,387

Note: income is shown net of rent and basic-rate tax.

Source: Age Concern/Hinton & Wild

However, outstanding debts (such as a mortgage) are knocked off the total first, so if you took out a £30,000 loan under plan 1, which must be repaid on death, the net loss to your heirs might be only £18,000.

Where to find advice and information
The charity Age Concern publishes an explanatory booklet on the schemes entitled *Using Your Home as Capital*. An organization

called Safe Home Income Plans (SHIP) also publishes some information leaflets on the schemes. (For addresses, see Appendix I, page 164). Member firms of SHIP maintain a code of conduct which states that no member can arrange a plan unless a client's solicitor has signed a certificate agreeing to the process.

Other ways of making your home pay for its keep
You might consider letting out a room on either a permanent or occasional basis. In either case, you should be able to benefit from the 'rent-a-room' tax relief, which allows income of up to £3,250 a year to be totally free of tax. If you expect to be earning significantly more than this, it may be worth consulting an accountant to establish whether 'rent-a-room' is still preferable to a normal let, which would allow you to claim against tax certain expenses involved in letting; with rent-a-room, no expenses are allowable.

13 | *Tax Planning*

This chapter deals with the main personal taxes, and how they affect people entering retirement. However, it is not a comprehensive tax textbook; anyone with complicated tax affairs should consult an accountant.

Income Tax

Income tax may have been introduced as a purely temporary measure to help pay for the Napoleonic wars, but no one would dispute that it is here to stay. The only consolation is that it is rather more fair to the majority of retired people than the alternative of 'invisible', indirect taxes on goods and services. Retired people tend to spend a greater proportion of their income than workers, so taxes on spending rather than income affect them unfairly.

Tax allowances
Everyone has the right to a certain level of income free of tax. These personal allowances are increased with age, as Table 21 shows. Thereafter, income is taxed at a rate which rises from 20% for the first slice of taxable income up to (currently) a maximum rate of 40%.

The age allowance 'trap'
The 'trap' operates because the higher amounts of age allowance for older ages are progressively withdrawn at the rate of £1 for every £2 of extra income above a certain threshold. This threshold is £14,600 for the year 1995–96 and £15,200 for 1996–97. Once the

Table 21: Tax allowances and tax rates, 1995–96 and 1996–97

Personal allowances

	Age at 5 April	1995–96	1996–97
Personal	under 65	£3,525	£3,765
	65–74	£4,630	£4,910
	75 and over	£4,800	£5,090
Married couple's	under 65	£1,720	£1,790
	65–74	£2,995	£3,115
	75 and over	£3,035	£3,155
Widow's		£1,720	£1,790

Note: the increased married couple's allowance is given for the year in which either partner has reached the relevant age. It is normally given to the husband but can be split equally or given all to the wife if they so choose. The widow's allowance (it is not given to widowers) applies for the year in which her husband dies and the following year. There are no age-related increases for this and the allowance only applies where the couple were living together before his death. Both married couple's and widow's allowances are restricted in value to 15% relief rather than the full 25%.

The age-related increases on personal allowances are progressively withdrawn once income exceeds a certain level (see below).

Income tax rates

1995–96		1996–97	
Rate of tax	Slice of taxable income	Rate of tax	Slice of taxable income
20%	£1–£3,200	20%	£1–£3,900
25%	£3,201–£24,300	24%	£3,901–£25,500
40%	over £24,300	40%	over £25,500

Note: from April 1996, basic-rate taxpayers will be liable to tax on interest earned from most types of savings at the lower rate of 20% only. However, higher-rate taxpayers must pay an additional 20% charge, bringing their rate up to the full 40%. Where people have both earned income (including pensions) and income from savings, the savings portion is treated as the 'top slice' of the total income.

personal allowance has been reduced to the normal (under 65) level, the taxmen then transfer their attention to the married couple's allowance, which in turn is whittled away at the same rate until it reaches the normal level.

The effect of this withdrawal is to impose an effective marginal tax rate of up to 37.5% on the slice of income immediately above £14,600, operating on the next £3,000- to £5,000-worth of annual income, depending on whether you are married or not, and above or below the age of 75.

The precise figures for the tax year 1995–96 and 1996–97 are as follows:

	1995–96	1996–97
Single person aged 65–74:	£14,600–£16,810	£15,200–£17,490
Married man aged 65–74:	£14,600–£19,360	£15,200–£20,140
Single person aged 75+:	£14,600–£17,150	£15,200–£17,850
Married man aged 75+:	£14,600–£19,780	£15,200–£20,580

For anyone whose retirement income is well above these levels, the whole of the extra allowances will be foregone and there is probably little that can be done in the way of planning.

However, if your joint incomes come to, say, £20,000, it may be worth trying to rearrange your affairs in order to preserve some of your increased allowances. Independent taxation means that both partners are entitled to personal allowances in their own right, so if – as is often the case – the bulk of the household income is in the form of the husband's pension, it may well be a good idea to put joint investments solely in the wife's name. So long as her income from these does not amount to more than £14,600 (1995–96) or £15,200 (1996–97), then she can retain her higher personal allowance – assuming, of course, she is aged 65 or more. In working out the figures, do not forget that a portion of the married man's basic State pension counts as his wife's income and, while this is paid gross, it is taxable.

Investments that might be transferred include anything producing taxable interest, such as building society accounts. In addition, make sure you are using the various tax-favoured investments, in particular Tessas and Peps, to the full. Income from these does not 'count' as income for age allowance purposes. While Pep income can be withdrawn at any time, remember that income from a Tessa may only be withdrawn during the term after a notional deduction of basic-rate tax (with the balance rolling up until the end of the period).

For those who do not wish to withdraw income, but want a safe 'nest egg', fixed interest National Savings Certificates, where the annual growth is tax-free, may be a useful alternative.

Income tax: planning pre-retirement

Employees who are within a year or so of retirement should make a mental note to take a look at their tax affairs as they enter their last tax year of employment. If you are retiring part way through a tax year, it is a good idea to write to your Inspector of Taxes a few months earlier asking for your coding to be amended from the date of retirement. Your income, of course, will change but, more to the point, retirement may signal the end of a host of 'taxable benefits', such as a company car, free petrol, and membership of a private medical insurance scheme. These can usually be 'apportioned' through the tax year, so if you give them up halfway through the year, you should only pay half the tax, which is achieved by an increase in your coding.

'Golden handshakes' and redundancy payments

The position here is fairly complicated and in some instances boils down to 'general practice' rather than clear-cut law. Statutory redundancy payments are definitely tax-free; additional redundancy payments may or may not be tax-free. There is a further rule that so-called 'golden handshakes' – compensation payments made on an *ex gratia* basis to people whose contract has been terminated early – can be tax-free up to £30,000 (although any statutory redundancy payments made at the same time must be deducted from this £30,000 total first), but if such payments are made in connection with your retirement, then they will generally be fully taxable as income arising in that year.

If this is the case, and it is possible to negotiate the timing, see if you can retire towards the beginning of a tax year and delay taking your pension during that year. This could mean the bulk of it will be taxed at 25%; otherwise the whole lot may be taxed at 40%. If the sums involved are substantial, it will undoubtedly pay you to take professional advice on the matter.

Payments for undertakings on future business

Some people may be retiring early from a company with plans to set up as an independent consultant in the same field. If your old company requires you, for example, not to offer your services to certain competitors for a certain period of time and pays you for that undertaking, then the payment counts as salary and is fully taxable.

Tax on investments

The previous chapters dealing with specific investments have already dealt with the taxation position of those investments, but it may be worth recapping on a few points:

Building society and bank interest: From April 1996, this will be normally paid out net of 20% tax and basic-rate taxpayers have no further liability. If you are a non-taxpayer, you can elect to receive the interest gross, without deduction, by filling in form R85, which is available from building societies, banks and local tax offices. If you have not made the election but you realize you could have done so, then you can reclaim the tax, which can be backdated to 6 April 1990, when the law changed. Higher-rate taxpayers must declare the gross interest received, and will in due course receive an extra tax bill for 20% of the gross.

Dividends from shares and unit trusts: Share dividends are also paid out net of a 20% tax charge. The basic-rate taxpayer has no further liability, but higher-rate taxpayers must pay an additional 20% on the gross amount. Non-taxpayers can reclaim the tax of 20%.

Income from pensions: All pensions from the State are paid out gross, but they are taxable. This rule applies to the basic old age pension, any graduated pension, and any Serps entitlement.

Other pension income, whether it comes from a company final salary-type pension or a personal pension, is all paid out net of basic-rate tax at 24%. This can be reclaimed by non-taxpayers, and attracts an extra charge in the hands of higher-rate taxpayers (16% of the gross).

Income arising from life assurance investments: This is generally free of tax for basic-rate taxpayers (though non-taxpayers cannot reclaim any), but higher-rate taxpayers generally face an extra charge.

Payments from ordinary life annuities: These are paid out net of 20% tax, which can be reclaimed by non-taxpayers and are subject to a further 20% tax on the interest portion of the payment from higher-rate taxpayers. Taxpayers liable to 25% tax have no further liability.

Gifts between husband and wife to take advantage of separate taxation: The Revenue accepts that couples may swap their assets around in order to gain the maximum advantage from the separate taxation rules, *but* such a rearrangement must reflect a genuine gift, with no strings attached. If it later emerges they were not really gifts, the Revenue could go back and ask for extra tax. Where assets are held jointly, the Revenue will treat the owner-ship as split 50:50, but you can opt for different proportions, for instance 70:30.

Capital Gains Tax

Capital gains tax (CGT) is in theory payable on all the profits realized by the sale of an investment, but there are two important qualifications to this general rule. First, every individual has an annual tax-free allowance (£6,000 in 1995–96 and £6,300 in 1996–97), so gains up to this amount can be realized tax-free. Larger total gains in any one year will be free of tax to the extent of this allowance with only the balance taxable. It is then taxed as if it is the 'top slice' of the investor's income for that year, which, depending on the level of their other income, may be at 20%, 24% (1996–97) or 40%.

The fact that every individual is allowed this annual exemption is a further inducement to split investments between husband and wife, so both can make use of the exemption. In addition, one of you may have a lower marginal income tax rate than the other, so gains above this limit could be taxed at a lower rate if they are in the right hands.

In addition, only 'real' gains are taxable – in other words, gains above inflation. The indexation provisions allow investors to inflate the purchase price of their investment by the total amount of inflation experienced since the asset was bought. Where the assets have been held for many years, investors can use the value of the asset at 31 March 1982 as the 'base cost', to which indexation for the following period may be added. In addition to the purchase price itself, investors can add in the costs of buying and selling it (for example, in the case of shares, stockbrokers' commission and stamp duty), and these in turn may also be indexed.

Any capital losses realized in the same tax year can be offset against total gains, reducing your potential tax bill. However, losses cannot now be indexed in the same way as gains: for example, if you bought some shares 10 years ago for £20,000 and you sell them today for the same amount of money, that represents quite a loss in real terms, but the taxman will not recognize it as a loss.

Gains can be 'realized' not just by selling assets, but by making an outright gift of them. However, gifts between husband and wife do not count in this respect. Assets passing on death are not liable to CGT, though they may be liable to inheritance tax (see below).

Exemptions from CGT

There are a small number of assets which are completely exempt from CGT. The main one is your home – your 'principal private residence' – but others include 'chattels' (defined as tangible movable property) sold for less than £6,000, motor cars, personal holdings of gilts – and, of course, gains arising from investments held in a Personal Equity Plan, which are tax-free. One word of warning: anyone who 'wheels and deals' on a regular basis, buying and selling things for profit, may be treated by the Revenue as 'trading', in which case profits may be subject to income tax.

Bed and breakfasting

The annual CGT exemption cannot be carried forward from one tax year to the next, so if you don't use it, you lose it. Hence the procedure known as 'bed and breakfasting', whereby investors sell a holding of shares, say, just before the end of the tax year, realizing profits within the CGT exemption, and buy them back the next day. This exercise costs money in terms of stockbrokers' commission (although some firms will do special cut-price deals for the joint operation) and, of course, you take the risk that the stock market will move against you between the day of sale and the day of purchase. But it does mean that you can avoid building up a big capital gain over the years.

CGT on monthly savings plans

Many investors have built up considerable capital over the years by making regular monthly payments into a unit trust or investment trust savings plan. In theory, in order to calculate the precise amount of any gain, one would have to index each monthly contribution separately, together with the associated purchase costs, but the Revenue allows investors to treat all their monthly payments within one year as a single purchase made in the seventh month of the trust's accounting year. This cuts down the number of individual calculations from 12 to one for each year, although it could still be a lengthy process.

CGT and the sale of a business

If you are selling your business on retirement, and are aged at least 50 then there are special concessions. Broadly speaking, the first £250,000 of gains are exempt, and half the balance up to £1m, as long as you have owned the business for the previous 10 years – shorter periods mean less relief. If the business is owned jointly by a married couple, both qualify individually for the exemption.

Inheritance Tax

Inheritance tax (IHT) may be payable both on gifts made during your life and also on assets passing after death. However, all assets passing between husband and wife, whether during life or at death, are free from IHT, but of course this does not cancel, but only delays, an eventual tax bill.

Attitudes to IHT vary considerably: some people think their children will benefit sufficiently to make the payment of IHT an acceptable price to pay; others are furious to think that so much of their hard-earned savings – the fruits, perhaps, of a lifetime of industry and careful living – should be grabbed by the Government after their death; yet more, one suspects, simply do not realize how much the IHT bill might be.

There is a nil rate band for IHT purposes which is £154,000 for the tax year 1995–96 and £200,000 for 1996–97. This means that assets up to this level can be given away without any IHT charge. But the balance of assets passing at death attracts tax at 40%. The other basic rules are as follows:

Gifts made during life

The following gifts are exempt from IHT:

- Up to £3,000 per year. If unused, this allowance may be carried forward, but for one year only.
- Small gifts of no more than £250 to each recipient per year.
- Gifts which form 'part of normal expenditure out of income'

(no precise monetary limit is placed here: it is generally taken to mean gifts of a regular nature which do not diminish your accustomed standard of living).

- Gifts of £5,000 on marriage (by parents), £2,500 (by grandparents) and £1,000 (by any other relative or friend).
- Gifts made by husband to wife or vice versa.
- Gifts to charities and political parties of any amount.

Other gifts – of whatever size – that are made during lifetime are known as Potentially Exempt Transfers (PETs). They are only potentially exempt because you have to live for a further seven years after making the gift for them to be wholly exempt; if you die before then there is a tapering charge, as follows:

Years between gift and death	% of full rate
0–3	100%
3–4	80%
4–5	60%
5–6	40%
6–7	20%

So if, for example, you made a PET of £10,000 and then died four and a bit years later, then (assuming it is not covered by the nil rate band) the IHT tax bill on this £10,000 would be £2,400 (at a rate of 25% – 60% of 40%.)

IHT and the family business

From April 1996, there will be 100% relief from IHT on transfers of shares in qualifying, unquoted companies – typically, the family business.

Ways of reducing IHT

There are some simple and obvious moves that you can make to cut down the eventual size of the IHT bill; others are neither simple nor obvious. There is a long-running guerrilla war between the Revenue and firms of tax-planners, as the latter devise schemes to avoid IHT and the Revenue catches up and slots in another anti-avoidance provision in the following budget. This means that you need to be extremely careful: it is all very well setting up some wonderful tax-planning scheme to work under current legislation, but there is no means of telling whether it will still be valid when you do eventually die.

Simple ways of cutting down IHT

Try to give away as much as you can during your lifetime, both by making use of the annual exemptions and the rules on PETs. Married couples should try not to leave everything they own to each other: while no IHT is payable immediately, it does mean that the first 'nil rate band' of £200,000 goes to 'waste'. If possible, ensure that at least part of it is used by willing some assets to children (or grandchildren). Remember that lifetime gifts have to be real gifts: the Revenue has a category called 'gifts with reservation' to cover situations where, for example, you give away your house but retain the right to live in it until you die, or give away investments but keep the right to the income they produce: for IHT purposes, these are not gifts at all.

IHT and the home

Many people who are not especially wealthy in their own right have houses which are worth as much as, or more than, the nil rate band, which means that any other assets they leave will be subject to the full 40% tax bite. One 'solution' – not a very appealing one – is to give your house to your children and pay them a full commercial rent for continuing to occupy it. At least this has the explicit approval of the Inland Revenue.

A second is to accept that some tax will be payable, and to provide your children with the means to pay it. The most popular course is to start a life assurance scheme (your premiums should, normally, come within the IHT exemption of 'normal expenditure out of income'), with the policy written in trust for the benefit of the children. This should ensure that, when you die, your heirs will have immediate access to a sum of money with which to pay, or help pay, the IHT bill. The usual policy taken out in these circumstances is a whole of life policy, but it could be term assurance. If you are married and wish to leave the house and most of your other assets to your partner, then the IHT reckoning is likely to come in only after the second death, so the life assurance policy could be written on a 'joint lives, last survivor' basis, paying out only after the second death.

People who have made significant PETs can take out specially designed term assurance policies lasting for seven years, designed to pay out a sum on death within the term that will match the current IHT liability.

Other schemes

Over the years, numerous other schemes to avoid IHT, generally life assurance products, have been devised: many make use of some form of trust, usually to allow people to give away assets during their lifetime, while retaining access to some sort of benefit connected with those assets (such as the right to obtain regular loans from the trust to use as income). Other schemes involving trusts have been devised to allow people to leave their half of the matrimonial home to their children, even if they die first.

This is a highly complex field where up-to-date and professional advice is absolutely essential. As noted above, the rules sometimes change from year to year, and in the last few years there appears to have been a general hardening in the Revenue's attitude. Some schemes have obtained counsel's opinion but have not yet been tested by the courts, so their efficacy remains unproven.

Deeds of variation

Given all the uncertainties, many people end up willing everything to their partner anyway, even though it is the least tax-efficient option. After all, how can people in their 60s, say, predict what their financial situation will be like in 20 years' time or whether their surviving spouse will be able to live reasonably on only half the joint assets?

At the present time there is a slight let-out: after someone's death a 'deed of variation' to the will can be executed. The deed must be signed by everyone who would have benefited under the terms of the original will and it can, in effect, simply rewrite the will. The deed must be completed within two years of death.

This means that your affairs can be rearranged in a much more tax-efficient manner, and the two-year time limit gives some scope for careful weighing of the options. However, your heirs *must* tell the tax authorities about the variation within six months of its execution.

14 | *Making a Will*

More than half the adults in this country have not got around to making a will, and retirement is an excellent time to put the matter right. The estate of anyone who dies without a valid will (or 'intestate') will be divided up under pre-set rules – which vary according to whether your home is in Scotland or England and Wales – but, of course, you will have no say in the matter.

The full intestacy provisions in England and Wales run to around half a dozen closely printed pages, but the basic rules are these:

- **If you are married with children:** the spouse gets the personal belongings, the first £125,000 absolutely, and a 'life interest' (the income but not the capital) on half of the rest. The children (in equal shares) get: the balance of half the rest, and the remainder of the estate when the survivor dies.
- **Married without children:** the spouse gets the personal belongings, the first £200,000 absolutely, and half the balance absolutely. The rest goes to relatives in a pecking order which starts with your parents, if they are alive; if they are not, it goes to your brothers and sisters or, if they are dead, to their children – in other words, your nephews and nieces. If there are none of these, the spouse receives everything absolutely.
- **Single person:** the estate goes to your children. If there are none, it goes to parents, if alive; if not, to brothers, sisters or nephews and nieces; otherwise, to grandparents, and finally to uncles and aunts (or their children). If you have no living relatives within these definitions, the whole estate goes to the Crown.

If you were living with someone, but not legally married, your partner has no rights under the intestacy laws, no matter how long you might have lived together.

In Scotland the position is quite different in that both spouse and children have certain specified rights to portions of your estate.

It would be unusual for the intestacy provisions to chime in exactly with an individual's wishes; even if they did, it still makes more sense to write a will because it should make the business of clearing up your estate that much quicker. In any case, if you wish to leave personal bequests – either particular items or monetary gifts to friends, relations or godchildren, for example – or if you wish to leave money to a specific charity, the only way of doing so is to make a will.

How to Make a will

There are three options: doing it yourself; using a will-writing agency; or using a solicitor. The DIY route is the cheapest, involving no more than a few pounds' expenditure on a special kit, including a draft will. However, the standard legal textbook on wills runs to 1,700 pages, so unless you are really confident that your affairs are straightforward, this may not be a sensible option. The alternatives, in any case, need not be terribly expensive.

A number of specialist will-writing agencies have grown up in recent years, providing a useful service. However, many are attached to insurance companies and you may find yourself on the receiving end of a sales pitch for some of the company's other products if you take this option.

Going to a solicitor is the most obvious choice, and would seem to be the most sensible for the vast majority of people. The cost will vary widely, principally according to the amount of time a solicitor has to spend on your case, so make sure that you are clear in your own mind what you wish the will to say otherwise you will end up wasting time (and money).

Legal requirements

In England and Wales there are few rules about who you must leave money to (unlike many other countries), but the law does try to ensure that families and dependants are adequately catered for. If a widow (or unmarried former wife), who was dependent on you immediately before your death, is cut out of the will or left an inadequate amount, she is entitled to go to the courts to ask for more. In Scotland the requirements are more complicated but just as strict.

Contents of the will

You can leave specific beneficiaries either a particular sum – say, '£10,000' – or a proportion of the estate ('50%'), or particular items ('my second best bed'). You will need to be quite careful if you are leaving specific large sums of money. Remember that inheritance tax must be paid out of the estate and, if the bill is large, you may end up leaving a greater proportion of your net assets to some individuals than you had intended. If you are leaving specific items to people, you may have to review your will in due course: you can't leave your Ming dynasty vase to a favourite niece if you subsequently get an offer you cannot refuse from an auctioneers. It is usual – and sensible – to name one person to receive a 'gift of residue' – any money or possessions left over after all the other bequests have been dealt with.

Signing of the will and storage

You need two people to witness your signature; they do not need to see its contents to do so. They must be people who will not benefit under the will. You must then decide where to keep it: you can store it with your bank or solicitor, for example, keeping a copy in your own possession. Do tell someone where it is – unless you are amused at the thought of your relatives rushing round the house in search of secret drawers, like a scene from an Ealing comedy.

Executors

You will need to decide who to appoint as your executors – the people who will be in charge of carrying out the will's instructions. Many people appoint two: a close relative, and a professional, such as a solicitor, but you are not obliged to. You could appoint your wife or husband as sole executor; he or she would then seek professional advice if necessary. If you wish, you can have as many as four executors.

Most of the high street banks have executor departments, and you can appoint one of these instead of a solicitor. Inevitably, this entails extra costs: solicitors tend to charge on the time taken; banks may charge on the basis of a percentage of the estate and, where your affairs are relatively simple, this may be an unnecessary expenditure.

Making it easy for them

Making matters easy for executors also means making things easy for yourself in the meantime. If your idea of planning is to throw everything into a shoebox, you will no doubt find the annual chore of filling out your tax return a complete nightmare. You could also be losing money – for example, by keeping out-of-date building society accounts paying poor rates of interest.

Now that you are about to retire, make a resolution to spend at least a day or two of your new freedom 'working': set up a simple filing system with clear records of what you own and where it is.

APPENDIX I
Useful Names and Addresses

The following organizations have been referred to in the text:

Regulatory Organizations

Securities and Investments Board
Gavrelle House
2–14 Bunhill Row
London EC1Y 8RA
0171 638 1230

Personal Investment Authority
Consumer Helpdesk
1 Canada Square
Canary Wharf
London E14 4AZ
0171 538 8860

Securities and Futures Authority
Cotton Centre
Cotton's Lane
London SE1 2QB
0171 378 9000

Insurance Brokers Registration Council
15 St Helens Place
London EC3A 6DS
0171 588 4387

Investment Managers Regulatory Organization
5th floor
Lloyd's Chambers
Portsoken Street
London E1 8BT
0171 390 5000

Pensions Organizations

OPAS
11 Belgrave Road
London SW1V 1RB
0171 233 8080

Pension Schemes Registry
PO Box 1NN
Newcastle-upon-Tyne
NE99 1NN
(Enquiries in writing only)

Pensions Ombudsman
11 Belgrave Road
London SW1V 1RB
0171 834 9144

Other Ombudsman Offices

Investment Ombudsman
6 Frederick's Place
London EC2R 8BT
0171 796 3065

Personal Investment Authority Ombudsman
3rd floor
Centrepoint
103 New Oxford Street
London WC1A 1QH
0171 379 0444

Insurance Ombudsman
City Gate One
135 Park Street
London SE1 9EA
0171 928 7600

Insurance

Age Concern Insurance Services
Garrard House
Chaldon Road
Caterham
Surrey CR3 5YZ
01883 346964

Retirement Insurance Advisory Service

Aspen House
37 Commercial Road
Poole
Dorset BH14 0HU
0800 552 100

Specialist Annuity Advisers

The Annuity Bureau
Enterprise House
59–65 Upper Ground
London SE1 9PQ
0171 620 4090

Annuity Direct
27 Paul Street
London EC2A 4JU
0171 588 9393

Directories of Independent Advisers

IFA Promotion
Studio House
5–7 Flowers Hill
Brislington
Bristol BS4 5JJ
0117 971 1177

National Directory of Fee-based Advisers
Matrix Data Services
Freepost
Gossard House
7–8 Savile Row
London W1X 1AF
(telephone enquiries to:
0117 976 9444)

Association of Private Client Investment Managers and Stockbrokers
(APCIMS)
112 Middlesex Street
London E1 7HY
0171 247 7080

Specialist Magazines

Money Management
3rd floor
Maple House
149 Tottenham Court Road
London W1P 9LL
0171 896 2525

Planned Savings
33–9 Bowling Green Lane
London EC1R 0DA
0181 956 3016 (subscriptions)

Moneyfacts
Laundry Loke
North Walsham
Norfolk NR28 0BD
01692 500765

PepGuide
Chase de Vere Investments
63 Lincoln's Inn Fields
London WC2A 3BR
0171 404 5766

Trade Bodies

Association of Investment Trust Companies
Durrant House
8–13 Chiswell Street
London EC1Y 4YY
0171 588 5347

Association of Unit Trusts and Investment Funds
65 Kingsway
London WC2B 6TD
0171 831 0898

Association of British Insurers
51 Gresham Street
London EC2V 7HQ
0171 600 3333

Charities

Age Concern England
1268 London Road
London SW16 4ER
0181 679 8000

Age Concern Cymru
4th floor
1 Cathedral Road
Cardiff CF1 9SD
01222 371 566

Age Concern Scotland
113 Rose Street
Edinburgh EH2 3DT
0131 220 3345

Age Concern Northern Ireland
3 Lower Crescent
Belfast BT7 1NR
01232 245729

Help the Aged
St James's Walk
Clerkenwell Green
London EC1R 0BE
0171 253 0253

Home Income Plans

Safe Home Income Plans
374–8 Ewell Road
Surbiton
Surrey KT6 7BB
0181 390 8166

Where to Buy Second-hand Endowment Policies

Association of Policy Marketmakers
Holywell Centre
1 Phipp Street
London EC2A 4PS
0171 739 3949

APPENDIX II
Special Courses on Pre-Retirement Planning

A number of colleges and adult education centres run courses on pre-retirement planning and preparation. There are also a number of commercial operations in this field, and many large companies provide places on such courses for their employees (and, often, their spouses as well). Such courses can last for an evening or a few days; they will cover many aspects of retirement, not just financial matters.

The Pre-Retirement Association, a registered charity, exists to raise standards in the education and training of pre-retirement advisers. It publishes an annual directory of course providers, which is available (price £8) from the address below. It also runs regular pre-retirement courses itself which are open to both individuals and companies which have a few employees approaching retirement. The cost for 1995 ranged from £130 + VAT (two days, non-residential) to £800 (two to three days, residential, for senior executives).

Individuals can join the PRA, entitling them to discounts on PRA publications and seminars, and copies of *Saga* magazine (10 times a year) and *Your Retirement* (annual).

Pre-Retirement Association
26 Frederick Sanger Road
Surrey Research Park
Guildford GU2 5YD
01483 301170

INDEX

The Sunday Times Personal Finance Guide to The Protection Game

A Straightforward Guide to Insurance

Kevin Pratt

Do you have adequate insurance protection and are you getting good value for your premiums?

The Protection Game covers the whole gamut of insurance products, from simple life cover, medical plans and income replacement schemes through to motor and household protection contracts. It is designed to help you build a portfolio of policies that will protect you and your family from the mishaps, misfortunes and tragedies that life so often has to offer.

This guide examines the various insurance policies on the market, describing how they are sold and what they are intended to cover. It cuts through the jargon that often surrounds this area and outlines why and how particular products are appropriate to particular circumstances. *The Protection Game* enables you to:

- remove the mystery and cut through the complexity of insurance
- discover where to get the best value for money
- protect your belongings, your home and your family
- find out what to do when things go wrong

In short, *The Protection Game* addresses everything you need to obtain the priceless gift of peace of mind.

0 00 638702 0

HarperCollinsPaperbacks

The Sunday Times Personal Finance Guide to Tax-free Savings

How to Make Your Money Work Hardest For You

Christopher Gilchrist

Are you making the most of your savings and investments?

Nobody enjoys paying tax but few people make full use of the many opportunities now available to everyone in the UK to save and invest tax-free. This guide explains the basics of tax and investment and shows how you can use tax-free plans to make more of your money, including:

- how moving your savings into tax-free schemes can boost your returns
- how to work out what you need to save for retirement and the best tax-exempt ways to do so
- the differences between lower-risk, moderate-risk and high-risk schemes and how much each could produce for you
- identifying the saving and investment plans that offer the best value for money
- the best plans for short-term and longer-term savings

Over a period of twenty years, £100 a month placed in a building society account might accumulate to £45,000. But a good tax-exempt savings plan linked to shares could turn that same £100 a month into £130,000.

Taking the right decisions now on where to save your surplus income could add tens of thousands of pounds to your personal wealth.

0 00 638703 9

HarperCollinsPaperbacks

The Sunday Times Personal Finance Guide to Your Home

How To Buy, Sell and Pay for It

Diana Wright

Are you thinking of buying a home?

- Should you choose a fixed or variable rate mortgage?
- Should you choose an endowment or Pep mortgage – or a simple repayment?
- How can you save money on insurance?
- How can you get out of negative equity?
- How do you get the best out of an estate agent?
- What is the best mortgage for a second-time buyer?

Your Home – How to Buy, Sell and Pay for It answers these questions and more in simple, jargon-free terms with plenty of clear examples to guide homebuyers – whether first-timers or those buying for the second or third time – through the jungle of competing mortgage, investment and insurance offers.

The book covers all aspects of mortgages – fixed and variable rates, cash-backs and discounts; it weighs up endowment and Pep mortgages, repayments and pension-linked schemes. It provides a simple guide to all insurance matters related to the home, and points the way to saving substantial sums by doing a bit of extra homework.

Buying a home involves the biggest financial decision most people are ever likely to make. This book will help you make the decision which might literally transform the rest of your financial life.

0 00 638704 7

HarperColllinsPaperbacks